S[illegible]IS N[illegible]NAL PARK AND EAST SUSSEX

Pathfinder® Guides

Outstanding Circular Walks

Revised by
Fiona Barltrop

Text:	David Hancock (2010 edition), including some revisions of original text supplied for *PFG More Sussex* and *PFG Surrey and Sussex* by Brian Conduit, John Brooks, Kevin Borman and Nick Channer. Revised text for 2020 edition, Fiona Barltrop
Photography:	David Hancock, Nick Channer, Crimson Publishing. Page 88, Fiona Barltrop. Front cover: © Kanuman/Shutterstock
Editorial:	Ark Creative (UK) Ltd
Design:	Ark Creative (UK) Ltd

ISBN: 978-0-31909-090-9

While every care has been taken to ensure the accuracy of the route directions, the publishers cannot accept responsibility for errors or omissions, or for changes in details given. The countryside is not static: hedges and fences can be removed, field boundaries can alter, stiles can be replaced by gates, footpaths can be rerouted and changes in ownership can result in the closure or diversion of some concessionary paths. Also, paths that are easy and pleasant for walking in fine conditions may become slippery, muddy and difficult in wet weather, while stepping stones across rivers and streams may become impassable.

If you find an inaccuracy in either the text or maps, please contact Trotman Publishing at the address below.

First published in Great Britain 2010 by Crimson Publishing and reprinted with amendments in 2015, 2017 and 2020.

This edition first published 2020 by Trotman Publishing. Reprinted 2021.

Trotman Publishing, 19-21D Charles Street, Bath, BA1 1HX
www.pathfinderwalks.co.uk

Printed in India by Replika Press Pvt. Ltd. 6/21

A catalogue record for this book is available from the British Library.

Front cover: The Seven Sisters and Coastguard Cottages from above Cuckmere Haven
Previous page: Pointing the way through the Rother Valley

Contents

Up to 2½ hours
Short walks

3–3½ hours
Half-day walks

4 hours and over
Longer, full-day walks

The walk times are provided as a guide only and are calculated using an average walking speed of 2½mph (4km/h), adding one minute for each 10m (33ft) of ascent, and then rounding the result to the nearest half hour.

Walks are considered to be dog friendly unless specified.

Keymap

CATERHAM
SEVENOAKS
Limpsfield
Westerham
Godstone
Oxted
Hurst Green
Bletchingley
Hildenborough
Edenbridge
Lingfield
Dormansland
Smallfield
Southborough
Felbridge
EAST GRINSTEAD
Copthorne
Blackham
Langton Green
Groombridge
Hartfield
Forest Row
Sharpthorne
Wych Cross
ASHDOWN FOREST
CROWBOROUGH
Balcombe
Ardingly
Danehill
Nutley
HAYWARDS HEATH
Lindfield
Maresfield
Fletching
Newick
UCKFIELD
BURGESS HILL
HEATHFIELD
LOW WEALD
Ditchling
Keymer
Plumpton
Barcombe
Ringmer
LEWES
Glynde
Falmer
Woodingdean
Saltdean
Rottingdean
Peacehaven
NEWHAVEN
SEAFORD
Polegate
Alfriston
Willingdon
East Dean
Birling Gap
BRIGHTON AND HOVE
South Downs Way

SCALE 1:280 000 or 1 INCH to about 4½ MILES 1CM to 2.8KM
0 2 4 6 8 10 KILOMETRES 15
0 2 4 6 MILES 8 10
KEYMAP HEIGHTS SHOWN IN METRES
LOW WEALD
Paddock Wood
Claygate
Marden
Staplehurst
Headcorn
Pluckley
Smarden
Frittenden
Bethersden
Horsmonden
Brenchley
Matfield
Goudhurst
Cranbrook
Sissinghurst Castle
Biddenden
High Halden
St Michaels
TENTERDEN
Woodchurch
Benenden
Hole Park
Rolvenden
Bedgebury Forest
Wadhurst
Ticehurst
Hawkhurst
Sandhurst
Newenden
Northiam
Great Dixter
Bodiam
Etchingham
Burwash
Robertsbridge
ISLE OF OXNEY
Wittersham
Stone in Oxney
Rother Levels
Iden
Peasmarsh
Beckley
RYE
Rye Harbour
Camber Castle
Winchelsea
Icklesham
Winchelsea Beach
Udimore
Brede
Sedlescombe
BATTLE
Westfield
Guestling Green
Pett
Fairlight
Cliff End
Fairlight Cove
Hollington
Ore
HASTINGS
St Leonards
Bulverhythe
BEXHILL
Cooden
Sidley
Hooe
Ninfield
Catsfield
Dallington
Brightling
Netherfield
Mountfield
Crowhurst
Telham
Herstmonceux
Windmill Hill
Wartling
Norman's Bay Sta
Pevensey Bay
Sovereign Harbour
Langney Point
EASTBOURNE
Royal Sovereign
A21
A28
A229
A259
A268
A262
A274
A2100
A271
A269
A228
A26
10
8
14
1
12
4
2
11
6
16

Walk	Page	Start	Nat. Grid Reference	Distance	Time	Height Gain
Airman's Grave and Duddleswell	16	Fairwarp church	TQ 465267	3½ miles (5.5km)	2 hrs	490ft (150m)
Alfriston, Long Man of Wilmington & Jevington	66	Alfriston	TQ 520031	8¼ miles (13.2km)	4 hrs	1,195ft (365m)
Arlington and Abbot's Wood	72	Arlington Reservoir	TQ 528074	8½ miles (13.6km)	4 hrs	375ft (115m)
Barcombe Mills and the Ouse Valley	20	Barcombe Mills	TQ 433146	4½ miles (7.2km)	2 hrs	n/a
Battle – 1066 Country Walk	14	Battle	TQ 748157	3½ miles (5.6km)	2 hrs	310ft (95m)
Beachy Head and Long Down	46	Old Lighthouse, nr. Beachy Head	TV 568954	6¾ miles (10.8km)	3½ hrs	870ft (265m)
Bewl Water from Wadhurst	32	Wadhurst	TQ 641317	5½ miles (8.8km)	3 hrs	590ft (180m)
Blackboys and Waldron	55	Blackboys	TQ 521208	7½ miles (12km)	3½ hrs	640ft (195m)
Blackcap and Stanmer Down from Ditchling	69	Ditchling Beacon	TQ 333129	8½ miles (13.7km)	4 hrs	900ft (275m)
Bodiam Castle and the Rother Valley	43	Bodiam	TQ 783254	7 miles (11.2km)	3½ hrs	490ft (150m)
Brightling Park and Fuller's Follies	18	Brightling	TQ 669202	4 miles (6.5km)	2 hrs	490ft (150m)
Burwash and Bateman's	28	Burwash	TQ 673246	5 miles (8km)	2½ hrs	525ft (160m)
Cuckmere Haven from Seaford	26	Seaford	TV 484985	4½ miles (7.2km)	2½ hrs	510ft (155m)
Cuckmere River and Norton Top from Alfriston	79	Alfriston	TQ 521032	9¼ miles (15km)	4½ hrs	770ft (235m)
Ditchling Beacon, Clayton Windmills & Chattri Memorial	86	Foot of Ditchling Beacon	TQ 325137	9 miles (14.5km)	5 hrs	1,565ft (475m)
Downland Walk from Telscombe	83	Telscombe	TQ 404032	9½ miles (15.3km)	4½ hrs	1,050ft (320m)
Firle Beacon and Charleston Farmhouse	30	Firle	TQ 469074	5 miles (8km)	2½ hrs	740ft (225m)
Friston Forest, the Seven Sisters & Cuckmere Haven	58	Exceat	TV 518994	6½ miles (10.5km)	3½ hrs	1,150ft (350m)
Groombridge – Through the Medway Valley	52	Groombridge	TQ 531373	7 miles (11.2km)	3½ hrs	720ft (220m)
Hartfield, Withyham and '500' Acre Wood	40	Hartfield	TQ 478359	6 miles (9.7km)	3 hrs	605ft (185m)
Herstmonceux	34	Herstmonceux	TQ 634125	5½ miles (8.9km)	3 hrs	560ft (170m)
Icklesham from Winchelsea	49	Winchelsea	TQ 905173	6¾ miles (10.8km)	3½ hrs	510ft (155m)
Lewes, Balmer Down and the River Ouse	89	Lewes	TQ 416104	12 miles (19.2km)	6 hrs	1,590ft (485m)
Mayfield and Wadhurst Park	62	Mayfield	TQ 587269	8¼ miles (13.2km)	4 hrs	870ft (265m)
Northiam and Great Dixter	12	Northiam	TQ 828245	3 miles (4.8km)	1½ hrs	215ft (65m)
Pevensey Levels	23	Pevensey	TQ 646048	5 miles (8km)	2 hrs	n/a
Rye from Iden	37	Iden church	TQ 915237	6 miles (9.7km)	3 hrs	310ft (95m)
Sussex Border Paths from Fletching	75	Fletching	TQ 429235	9¼ miles (15km)	4½ hrs	705ft (215m)

Comments

This Wealden walk illustrates two aspects of Ashdown Forest: the sandy heathland for the outward part and varied woodland for the return. It also visits the scene of a 1941 air crash.

A grand scenic walk on the South Downs that gives fine views of the Long Man of Wilmington, an ancient and intriguing chalk figure.

An easy, level walk through the Cuckmere Valley from Arlington Reservoir, a favoured local picnic and birdwatching spot. The walk passes 13th-century Michelham Priory and explores Abbot's Wood.

With the riverside Anchor Inn close to the halfway point, this short and easy stroll through the Ouse Valley from pretty Barcombe Mills is perfect for a summer's evening outing.

Most people visit Battle to view the battlefield from the Abbey grounds. Fighting also took place on the land covered by part of this short walk, which uses paths through fields and woodland.

The South Downs Way has many stretches of exhilarating walking, but nowhere is it more spectacular than here. The outward route uses field paths and tracks to cross Long Down.

The walk follows the southern (Sussex) shore of the reservoir, the largest expanse of open water in southern England. Part of the route is underwalked and may be encroached by brambles and nettles.

A rural ramble through peaceful, gently undulating Wealden countryside to the tucked away village of Waldron. Woodland and field paths lead back to the famous Blackboys Inn for a well-earned drink.

This downland walk needs careful wayfaring as part of the route lacks signposts and the paths are sometimes vague. Much of the going is on springy turf while field paths and farm tracks are also used.

A glorious walk through orchards and fields in the Rother Valley from an evocative battlemented castle. Sunken Udiam Lane can be wet/muddy in winter but stunning Wealden views await near the top.

A short and very rewarding walk through Brightling Park, taking in 'Mad Jack' Fuller's fantastic follies and some magnificent Wealden views.

Holton Lane on the outward section is used by horses and may be muddy. This is the only drawback to a walk that encompasses the countryside surrounding Bateman's, once the home of Rudyard Kipling.

Seaford was once fashionable as a resort but its grand hotels went long ago. Its shore is still attractive as is the path that climbs steeply to Seaford Head, a magnificent viewpoint for the Seven Sisters.

The walk starts from Alfriston and climbs from the river to the top of the Downs above Seaford. The return descends the north-facing slope to visit Alciston and Berwick, where there are village inns.

There are splendid views from Ditchling Beacon and visits to the distinctive landmark windmills, Jack and Jill, and the Chattri Indian War Memorial, a very atmospheric spot on the Downs.

Many delightful villages are hidden in the downs, but none is more attractive than Telscombe. The route stays on top of the downs for its entire distance so be sure to take food and drink.

Take in far-reaching Wealden views from Firle Beacon and visit Charleston Farmhouse, former home to the Bloomsbury Set, before refuelling at the excellent Ram Inn.

A varied walk through forest, across downland, along cliffs and by a river estuary. The most spectacular stretch is across the chalk cliffs of the Seven Sisters.

After a brief foray into Kent, via Groombridge Place and a classic village green, this walk explores the lush, rolling Medway Valley landscape, returning along a disused railway trail – The Forest Way.

A walk in the 'Winnie the Pooh Country' of Ashdown Forest, going through part of Five Hundred Acre Wood and crossing 'Pooh Bridge'.

The footpath from the village to the castle gives views over the Pevensey Levels and also allows a glimpse of Herstmonceux Place, an 18th-century house built of bricks made from a Tudor castle.

Winchelsea, perched on its hilltop, is a unique town with a violent history. Its prosperity ended when the sea retreated. The walk explores the contrasting countryside to the west, notable for its orchards.

The route winds through Lewes at the start but soon climbs to the Downs and follows the South Downs Way northwards across lonely countryside before turning away to the east to Offham.

From pretty Mayfield the walk explores peaceful High Weald valleys, once thriving with iron smelting furnaces, and hidden away Wadhurst Park with its vast lake and deer herd.

The focus of this easy Wealden ramble is Great Dixter House, the former home of garden designer Christopher Lloyd, and its impressive and beautiful garden.

The Pevensey Levels are in low-lying pastures where it is difficult to avoid cattle. You will be rewarded by lonely, beautiful countryside, which is a delight to botanists and birdwatchers.

Not only is this a scenically rewarding walk that gives superb views of Rye, but there are also advantages in not having to take a car into the town where parking is difficult at peak times.

A National Trust garden, a trip along the Bluebell steam railway line, and a rural farm museum will encourage you to make a day of it following this rewarding ramble through rolling Wealden countryside.

Introduction to East Sussex & the South Downs

Tucked away in the far south-eastern corner of the country, just 40 miles (64km) south of London, East Sussex is often perceived as being one of the quintessential commuter counties: affluent, over-populated and criss-crossed by busy railway lines and congested roads leading to the capital. In this view, a diminishing amount of countryside is being gradually engulfed by a rising tide of bricks, concrete and tarmac. As is so often the case, the image does not match the reality and a number of popular misconceptions about the county need to be eliminated.

Unspoilt county

First, despite the county's proximity to London, the M25 and Gatwick Airport, there is perhaps a surprising amount of open, unspoilt and varied countryside left. Indeed, walkers in many parts of East Sussex may find themselves treading some of the quietest and loneliest footpaths in southern England.

Second, although far removed from the areas of traditional heavy industry, this was once England's major iron-producing area, the 'Black Country' of the Tudor and Stuart eras. Absence of local coal resources meant that the Industrial Revolution passed it by and little remains of its earlier industrial heritage, apart from some fine ironmasters' houses, including Rudyard Kipling's former home at Bateman's, and the numerous hammer ponds that are scattered throughout the Sussex Weald.

Third, for an area lying between the capital and the south coast noted for its prosperity and extensive communications network, it is hard to believe that it was once wild and remote. Weald actually means 'forest', and the region was originally a vast oak forest, forming a natural obstacle to progress northwards from the coast until the Romans built roads through it from Chichester to Lewes. Settlement followed, but even in Norman times the forest was still largely intact. In late medieval times, however, the oak trees began to be felled for charcoal that fuelled furnaces and made metal from local ironstone. In the 17th and 18th centuries yet more mature trees were cut down to build battleships and to construct the many fine timber-framed cottages to be seen in the county.

For the walker

East Sussex possesses a rich variety of scenery and terrain to satisfy every type of personality or mood, from the open ridge-tops of the South Downs, Britain's newest National Park, to the creeks and marshes around Rye Harbour, from the tree-clad slopes of the High Weald to the dramatic cliffs near Hastings, and from the wild heathland of the Ashdown Forest to the gentle river valleys of the Low Weald. East Sussex has a dense network of public footpaths and bridleways, supplemented by country parks and extensive areas owned by the National Trust. East Sussex is also criss-crossed by a number of long-distance and recreational paths. Foremost among these is the South Downs Way, one of Britain's premier national trails, which runs like a thread for 100 miles (160km) along the crest of the South Downs. Other trails include the 83-mile (133km) Wealdway and the 66-mile (106km) Vanguard Way, both of which traverse Ashdown Forest and pass through the Cuckmere Valley, the former heading to Beachy Head and Eastbourne, the latter to Seaford and Newhaven. Another favourite is the 150-mile (240km) Sussex Border Path, which was opened in 1980 and meanders through remote and peaceful countryside along the boundary between East and West Sussex. Other trails incorporated into the circular walks featured in this book include the High Weald Landscape Trail, a 90-mile (144km) route linking Horsham with Rye; the level Forest Way, which follows the route of a disused railway line for 10 miles (16km) between Forest Row and Groombridge; the glorious 1066 Walk, a 31-mile (50km) walk between Rye and Pevensey; and the Sussex Ouse Valley Way, which follows the river from its source near Lower Beeding in West Sussex to Seaford Bay. All are generally well maintained and waymarked to aid route finding.

Wealden views near Firle Beacon

The face of the county

The dominant geographical feature, stretching like a finger across Sussex from west to east, is the South Downs, their steep escarpment looking inward over the Weald. Exhibiting all the finest characteristics of chalk downland scenery, with smooth and rolling contours, short and springy turf and wonderful open vistas, they sweep across Sussex to terminate at Beachy Head and the spectacular Seven Sisters cliffs west of Eastbourne. Unsurprisingly, it is still the downland, with its rolling panoramas and exhilarating air, that attracts most walkers to East Sussex even though it is an area that covers only a small proportion of the county.

Most come to hike the South Downs Way, which follows ancient tracks along its ridge and the section through East Sussex is true open downland, bare and exposed, with glorious views north across the Weald and south over the Channel. Although the walker is never far from attractive villages and civilised amenities there is a great sense of spaciousness and some sections are really quite remote. The rivers Ouse and Cuckmere make spectacular sights from above as they meander in huge ox bow patterns to the sea, and there is a magnificent climax to the trail in East Sussex as it follows the swooping cliff-tops by Birling Gap, Seven Sisters and Beachy Head. A good clutch of exhilarating walks explore the best of the East Sussex downland, linking the South Downs Way with lonely, undulating tracks and bridleways, and visiting some key landmarks along the way, from Ditchling Beacon, the third highest point on the South Downs, and the 19th-century Clayton windmills, to Alfriston church, the 'cathedral of the downs', and the mysterious chalk carving known as the Long Man of Wilmington.

Elsewhere, a Wealden landscape predominates, a complex and scenically varied area of sandstone and clay, once covered by the vast, ancient forest of Andredesweald. The sandstone uplands of the High Weald reach up to 732 feet (223m) amid the birch, pine and open and breezy heathland of the Ashdown Forest, giving a type of walking along sandy tracks through heather and gorse that is surprising – sometimes in these parts there is the scenic flavour of a grouse moor and this is best experienced on the short walk from Fairwarp church. Tucked away, steep-sided valleys with streams that once provided power for the ironmasters' hammers are explored on walks from the ridge-top villages of Mayfield and Burwash, and the walk from Hartfield takes you through some of the remaining tracts of woodland, notably Five Hundred Acre Wood, made famous in A.A. Milne's *Winnie the Pooh* books.

The High Weald meets the English Channel to the east of Hastings, producing some of the finest cliff scenery on the south coast. From the many vantage points, grand views extend across the flatter, clay lands of the Low Weald; here is what many would claim to be the archetypal Wealden landscape of wide vistas, lazily meandering rivers, farms, woodland and idyllic villages of tile-hung houses and spacious greens. Rambles from Fletching, Blackboys, Arlington, Herstmonceux, Barcombe Mills and Bodiam explore this classic Wealden countryside.

Apart from the chalk cliffs where the South Downs meet the sea and the sandstone cliffs near Hastings, the East Sussex coast is fairly flat. A combination of easy access to London and a relatively dry and warm climate gave rise to some of England's earliest and best-known holiday resorts, notably Seaford, Eastbourne and Hastings. However, outside the built-up areas can be found an atmospheric and often haunting landscape of lonely marshlands, winding creeks and distant horizons, frequented more by the naturalist and ornithologist but not to be ignored by the walker, whose first thought might be to head for the downs. Walks among these coastal lowlands across the Pevensey Levels and over the reclaimed marshes near Rye are featured, as well as more energetic and dramatic cliff walks in and around the Seven Sisters Country Park.

Historical perspective

The most constant historical theme of East Sussex has been the threat of invasion from across the Channel, and throughout the county there are many reminders of this threat from the Roman period onwards. As Roman power dwindled and Anglo-Saxon attacks on the English coast intensified, the Romans built a chain of forts, 'Forts of the Saxon Shore', in an attempt to keep the invaders at bay. An outstanding example is explored on Walk 6 at Pevensey, part of which was later incorporated into a Norman castle. The forts, however, were a failure; the Saxons penetrated the region and created Sussex, or 'kingdom of the South Saxons'.

East Sussex witnessed the best known and indeed the last successful invasion of England in 1066 and Battle Abbey, built on the site of the decisive battle to commemorate the bloody encounter, is a reminder of the Norman Conquest. The short Walk 2 begins from abbey and crosses the battlefield. To consolidate their conquest and protect this highly vulnerable region between London and the south coast, the Normans built a series of castles at strategic locations on the main river routes across Sussex, as at Lewes on the River Ouse, which can be visited on Walk 28 from the town. Constant wars or threat of wars between England and France caused later medieval monarchs to create the federation of the Cinque Ports – five (later seven) towns on the Kent and Sussex coasts entrusted with the task of providing men and ships for the defence of the Channel in return for certain privileges. Hastings, Winchelsea and Rye were among the members and the latter two offer great interest to the visitor and are explored in this collection of walks.

South Downs National Park

They say life is full of coincidences. Within hours of the walks described in this guide being completed, the Government made a formal announcement that the South Downs of Sussex were at last to be given formal National Park status after a 60-year delay. The walking country that lies within the boundaries of the new park is key to the enjoyment of this book. But, above all, the guide's objective is to highlight the unique variety and enormous diversity of this special region of southern England and provide many hours of exercise and pleasure in the beautiful surroundings of East Sussex.

This book includes a list of waypoints alongside the description of the walk, so that you can enjoy the full benefits of gps should you wish to. For more information about route navigation, improving your map reading ability, walking with a GPS and for an introduction to basic map and compass techniques, read Pathfinder® Guide *Navigation Skills for Walkers* by outdoor writer Terry Marsh (ISBN 978-0-319-09175-3). This title is available in bookshops and online at os.uk/shop

Northiam and Great Dixter

Start	Northiam
Distance	3 miles (4.8km)
Height gain	215 feet (65m)
Approximate time	1½ hours (longer if visiting Great Dixter Gardens)
Parking	St Mary's Church car park
Route terrain	Field paths and village lanes
Ordnance Survey maps	Landranger 199 (Eastbourne & Hastings), Explorer 125 (Romney Marsh, Rye & Winchelsea)

GPS waypoints

- Start: TQ 828 245
- A: TQ 823 244
- B: TQ 810 247
- C: TQ 819 251
- D: TQ 830 250

A delightful walk close to the Kent/Sussex border, following the Sussex Border Path through gently rolling countryside to Great Dixter, a timbered 15th-century house surrounded by stunning gardens created by the late Christopher Lloyd, and the focus of the walk. The shorter return walk skirts the village centre and crosses fields, with lovely Rother Valley views, to St Mary's Church.

Northiam is a long straggling village lined with white weather-boarded cottages and where, according to legend, Queen Elizabeth I dined under an ancient oak on the village green in 1573 on her way to Rye.

Start: Turn left out of the car park, then left again along the main road and cross over in a few paces to follow the waymarked Sussex Border Path down a gravel drive between houses. At its end, keep left along the field edge to cross a footbridge and continue ahead in the next field, walking beside the right-hand hedge. Where the hedge ends, strike out across the centre of the field on a worn path to a T-junction of paths A.

Turn left, climb a stile in the hedge and continue down towards a house and a stile. Join an enclosed path that passes to the right of the house down to the driveway to Strawberry Hole. Turn right, cross the lane ahead and the stile opposite and follow the Sussex Border Path through pasture at the bottom of a shallow valley. Cross a stile and then a footbridge and turn immediately right along the field edge to reach another footbridge. Cross the bridge, walk across the next field and go through a copse, then follow the path right and keep to the field edge to reach another

Summer scene at Northiam

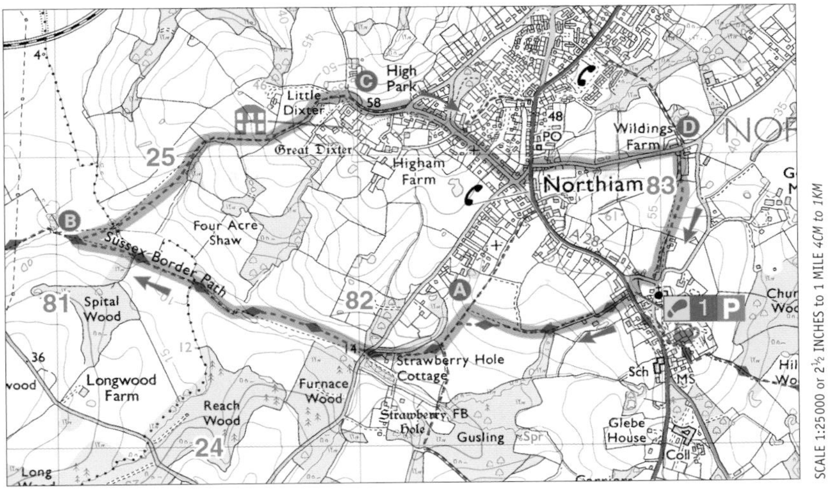

footbridge and a junction of paths **B**.

Turn right over the bridge and continue straight ahead, following the defined path gently uphill to a plank bridge and stile. Keep to the right-hand field edge uphill to cross a further stile by a gate, then keep to the grassy path as it skirts the gardens at Great Dixter, with fine views across the Rother Valley to your left. Skirt a small plantation and keep to the field edge as it bears right to a stile. Follow the drive ahead to reach the entrance to Great Dixter **C**.

The fine timber-framed Wealden hall house dates back to 1640 and is one of the county's smaller and more intimate historic houses. It was restored and enlarged by Sir Edward Lutyens in 1911 and was the home of the late Christopher Lloyd, the gardening writer, who died in 2006, and today the beautiful gardens are now the hallmark of this famous gardening expert. The impressive garden is in the Arts and Crafts style, and features topiary, an exciting and very colourful long border, an orchard and a glorious wild flower meadow, all of which surround the house. The planting is profuse, yet structured, and has featured many bold experiments of form, colour and

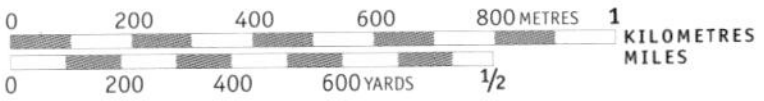

combination. Spend time exploring the garden; **teas and light refreshments** are served in the **gift shop** with seating in the garden.

Pass the toilets and join a narrow hedged path on the left that runs parallel with the metalled drive. At a junction of lanes on the edge of Northiam, follow Dixter Road ahead, passing the Unitarian Chapel on the right, to reach another road junction close to the A28. Turn left along Thyssel Lane and cross the A28 into Wildings Lane, walking along the road to a converted thatched barn on the left **D**.

Go through the gate opposite, beside the drive to Wildings Farm, and follow the fenced path to a kissing-gate. Walk across the field towards Northiam church, go through a gate and keep to the left-hand field edge to a further gate and lane, with St Mary's Church away to your left. The church deserves closer inspection as it dates from the 12th century and has a tall tower surmounted by a rare 16th-century octagonal stone spire. Turn right and follow the lane back to the car park. ●

Battle – 1066 Country Walk

Start	Battle Abbey gate
Distance	3½ miles (5.6km)
Height gain	310 feet (95m)
Approximate time	2 hours
Parking	Car park next to Abbey (Pay and Display)
Route terrain	Field and woodland paths; tarmac drives
Ordnance Survey maps	Landranger 199 (Eastbourne & Hastings), Explorer 124 (Hastings & Bexhill)

GPS waypoints

Start	TQ 748 157
A	TQ 742 155
B	TQ 737 149
C	TQ 741 138
D	TQ 744 140
E	TQ 744 147

This is a delightful short walk given extra interest in that it covers ground where fighting took place on 14 October, 1066. The longer trail taking this name extends from Rye to Pevensey, a distance of 31 miles (50km).

After his victory at the Battle of Hastings in 1066 King William gave thanks by founding an abbey at Battle, the high altar being erected at the spot where Harold fell. The site has belonged to English Heritage since 1976 when it was generously given to this country by the citizens of the United States in celebration of the bicentenary of their nation. Visitors can view the battlefield from the high ground now occupied by the abbey which was the position held by the Saxon army. The stream at the bottom of the little valley takes its reddish colour from iron in the bedrock, though tradition has it that this

Battle Abbey Gatehouse

commemorates the blood shed in the conflict. Once the abbey was established a town grew up around it, steadily increasing in size and prosperity as the monastery itself became increasingly rich and powerful.

Leave the car park by the abbey and turn left down a short lane that ends at a gate. Go through the gate and bear left to continue on the track that follows the fence around the wooded grounds of the abbey. When the path splits Ⓐ, keep right following the 1066 Country Walk. The path drops down towards woods.

After a pleasant stretch through conifers you come to a gate just before a cottage. There is a stile on the left 20 yards farther on Ⓑ. Go over the stile and cross a meadow to a stile into the wood. The path drops to a lake. You will see from the map that the **Powder Mills Hotel** is close by. Its name is taken from the gunpowder industry established in Battle in 1676 which lasted for almost 200 years before closing as fear grew for the safety of the town.

Cross the bridge at the outlet and climb ahead following a 'short walk' waymark. A short length of concrete track leads steeply uphill. At the top continue ahead to the road and cross it to the drive to Millers Farm.

Enjoy the views over lovely countryside, walking on the drive past an oast and farmhouse. After Badger's Keep, go through two galvanised gates Ⓒ, keep left along the front of the house and make for a stile ahead in the far boundary. Turn right and go down the pasture to a bridge and stile. Keep ahead on a bank that takes the path to a stile and metalled bridleway. Turn left, pass Stone Cottage Ⓓ and turn left again at a lane to reach a junction. Cross the road carefully to a stile and path opposite that runs above the road and parallel to it. At the top cross a track Ⓔ via stiles and then follow the track ahead down a gentle slope. Keep right at a fork, go through a gate and climb by the side of trees to reach the signpost at Ⓐ. Retrace your steps back to the imposing abbey gateway. ●

0 200 400 600 800 METRES 1 KILOMETRES
0 200 400 600 YARDS ½ MILES

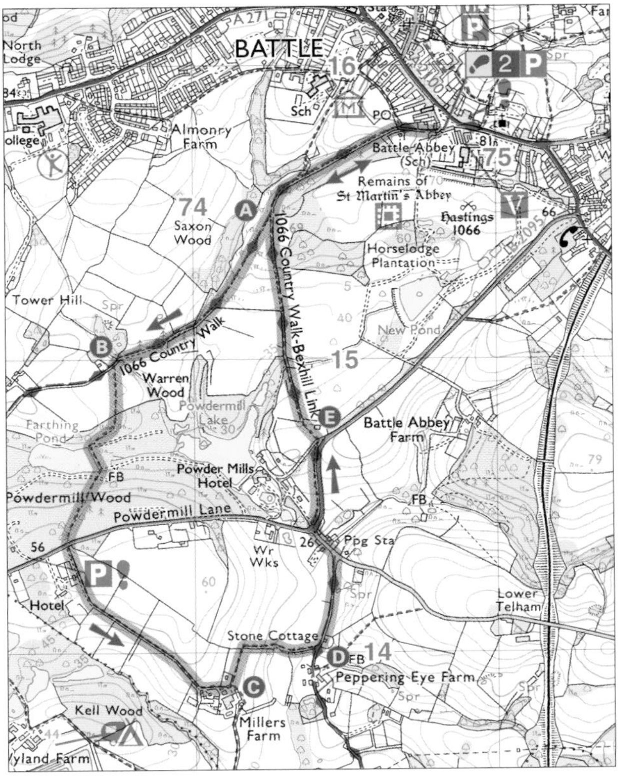

SCALE 1:25000 or 2½ INCHES to 1 MILE 4CM to 1KM

Airman's Grave and Duddleswell

Start	Fairwarp church (on B2026 north of Uckfield)
Distance	3½ miles (5.5km)
Height gain	490 feet (150m)
Approximate time	2 hours
Parking	Car park at the church. On Saturdays and Sundays when there are services it may be necessary to start the walk in the village, where there is on-road parking by the green
Route terrain	Heathland and woodland
Ordnance Survey maps	Landranger 198 (Brighton & Lewes), Explorer 135 (Ashdown Forest)

GPS waypoints

- TQ 465 267
- Ⓐ TQ 458 274
- Ⓑ TQ 462 286
- Ⓒ TQ 469 279
- Ⓓ TQ 471 274
- Ⓔ TQ 471 269

The first half of this walk in Ashdown Forest is over sandy heath, not at all like a forest. However, the return is through proper woodland, and it is easy to understand why this part of the High Weald is designated an Area of Outstanding Natural Beauty.

Fairwarp is a comparatively new village. When the name was first recorded in 1777 there was just a single farmhouse on the spot, but expansion came in the second half of the 19th century, the church being consecrated in 1881. Although the village remains active and prosperous, the latter years of the 20th century saw it lose its school and post office. Fortunately, the pub – appropriately the **Foresters' Arms** – survives.

The path at the far end of the car park leads to a T-junction. Turn left past the east end of the church and fork right at a grassy area to come to a crossways. Turn left, following the waymark of Maresfield Millennium Footpath. Cross the road to the track going to Spring Garden Farm, bearing to the right through a gate to follow a Millenium Footpath sign. The way across the heath is gloriously colourful at most times of the year with heather, bracken, gorse and birch. Keep ahead at a crossways and continue ahead at a junction where a farmyard is to the left. The way heads downhill in a north-westerly direction, and Nutley can be seen on the other side of the little valley – there is a Scottish (or at least Peak District) feel to this part of the walk as the path comes to a ford Ⓐ, although the water here is far from that of a pure Highland stream.

Turn right and climb to pass the stone enclosure that protects the grave of the Second Pilot of a Wellington bomber that crashed here on 31 July, 1941. The names of the six members of its crew are inscribed on a memorial. From here the path climbs gently to a car park and a road Ⓑ.

Turn right just before the road, and continue climbing for about 250 yards past the summit. Fork left where the track curves right and follow a narrow path through high bracken in season, keeping close to the heathland edge and passing stables away to the left. Continue through light woodland to a fork near a metal gate; bear left onto a narrower, more indistinct path, keeping close to the woodland fringe on your left until you cross a plank bridge and come to the B2026.

From here the popular **Duddleswell Tearooms** *are just 200 yards down the road on your right.*

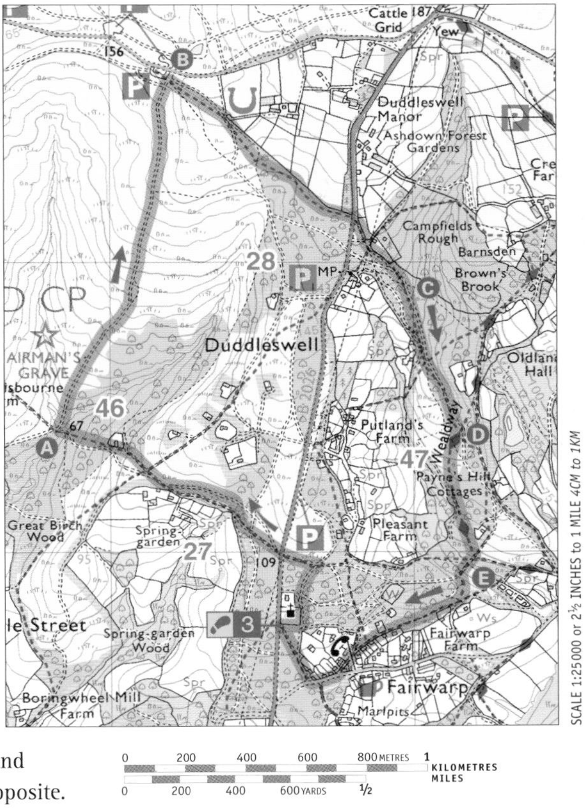

Cross this busy main road, and continue down the footpath opposite. Zigzag left and right across the drive to a house, and continue through the woods ahead when the path meets a wider grassy track Ⓒ.

The walking is easy as the track passes a drive on the right, and a 'WW' post on a right-hand bend shows where the Weald Way joins the route Ⓓ.

Pass a white cottage on the left and fork right when the track divides to cross another track after about 100 yards. The track swings right and drops to a shady bridge over a tiny stream. Climb the hill on the other side but, after 50 yards and just before the brow of the hill, go left Ⓔ on a lesser path, which climbs through bracken and birch. Fork left as the path levels out and comes to a grassy area in front of a white, weather-boarded house. Turn right to walk with the hedge around the next property, close on the left, to reach a path ahead through bracken that soon reaches an unmade road. Join this road, which leads to the village green at Fairwarp, with the Foresters' Arms along the road to your left.

Turn right and, at the end of the green, go right again on a track past the last houses in the village. After 100 yards fork left onto a footpath that leads directly to the starting point of the walk at Fairwarp church. ●

Towards Nutley

Brightling Park and Fuller's Follies

Start	Brightling
Distance	4 miles (6.5km)
Height gain	490 feet (150m)
Approximate time	2 hours
Parking	Forestry Commission car park on west side of Brightling Park
Route terrain	Field, parkland and woodland paths
Ordnance Survey maps	Landranger 198 (Brighton & Lewes), Explorer 135 (Ashdown Forest)

GPS waypoints

- Start: TQ 669 202
- A TQ 676 207
- B TQ 683 210
- C TQ 686 206
- D TQ 675 199
- E TQ 671 198
- F TQ 669 195

This glorious short walk explores the peaceful paths and bridleways through Brightling Park and 'Mad Jack' Fuller's fantastic 19th-century follies, the route taking you to the Sugar Loaf for stunning Wealden views, and Fuller's final folly, his sandstone pyramid mausoleum in Brightling churchyard.

Scattered around the hills and parkland surrounding Brightling is a strange collection of monuments and follies, including an obelisk, tower and peculiar cone known as the Sugar Loaf, built by the 19th-century eccentric 'Mad Jack' Fuller, the local squire, ironmaster and MP who resided in Brightling Park.

Take the forest track beyond the barrier past the Forestry Commission's Deer Park sign and gently descend to reach a crossing of paths after 250 yards. Follow the white arrow left, the path dipping and climbing through beech trees and gently bearing right. At a fork/T-junction bear left and just a few paces beyond turn right as indicated by a white arrow. Follow the narrow path through the wood via a footbridge and marker post to reach a kissing-gate. Go through this leaving the wood (permissive access route) and keep to the right-hand field edge, going through a gate in the field corner and continuing to the next one. Turn right through this keeping ahead along the short track to enter Brightling Park **A**.

With views across the park, forest and the Sussex Weald, bear left and keep beside the ditch at the top edge of the park. Follow it as it curves left and cross the ditch to follow a path through a belt of trees and across The Avenue to enter a field with horse jumps and far-reaching views north across the High Weald. Bear right to a gate in the park wall and keep right along the lane to reach Brightling church **B**.

Go through a gate and walk through the churchyard, passing Fuller's Pyramid Mausoleum, and return to the road. Fuller died in 1834 and was buried beneath the floor of the 25-foot (7.6m) high pyramid, contrary to legend stating he was seated, dressed for dinner, wearing a top hat and holding a bottle of claret.

Turn right, then at a road junction on the left, signed to Robertsbridge, go through the kissing-gate ahead to follow the path down the left-hand edge of a field to a gate. Go across the next field, go through a gate and follow an enclosed path, which can be overgrown. Just after the next gate, climb the stile on the right and follow the fence ahead towards the Tower. It is thought that Fuller erected this battlemented tower so he could view Bodiam Castle, which he bought in 1828 for 3,000 guineas to save it from destruction. Cross the stile on the right before the trees and turn left passing to the right of the tower and descending to a stile and the road. Turn right and soon left (signed Ox Lodge) to join a track **C**.

Walk downhill, the path curving left between ponds to reach a fork of paths just beyond the cricket ground. Turn right, signed to The Sugar Loaf, and follow the track between barns to a stile and gate on the left just before a gate. Follow the path along the right-hand edge of the field, continuing into the next. At a gate on the right before you enter the woodland ahead, there's a good view of the Brightling Park Temple, reputedly built by Fuller for gambling sessions and entertaining ladies. Continue down through the copse, along a field edge and through a field and down into Marisbrook Wood. Turn right at a track and climb to a T-junction of tracks **D**.

Turn left to follow a grassy path through mixed woodland, ignoring the track on the right **E**, to reach a barrier at the woodland edge. At the road, turn immediately left into the drive to a reclamation yard, soon to bear off right along an enclosed path, signed to the Sugar Loaf. Go through a gate and walk across the field to the folly **F**, which is 35 feet (10.7m) tall.

Retrace your steps back into the woodland and walk back along the track for a few paces before taking the arrowed path left into the trees. The path runs parallel with the road back to the car park. ●

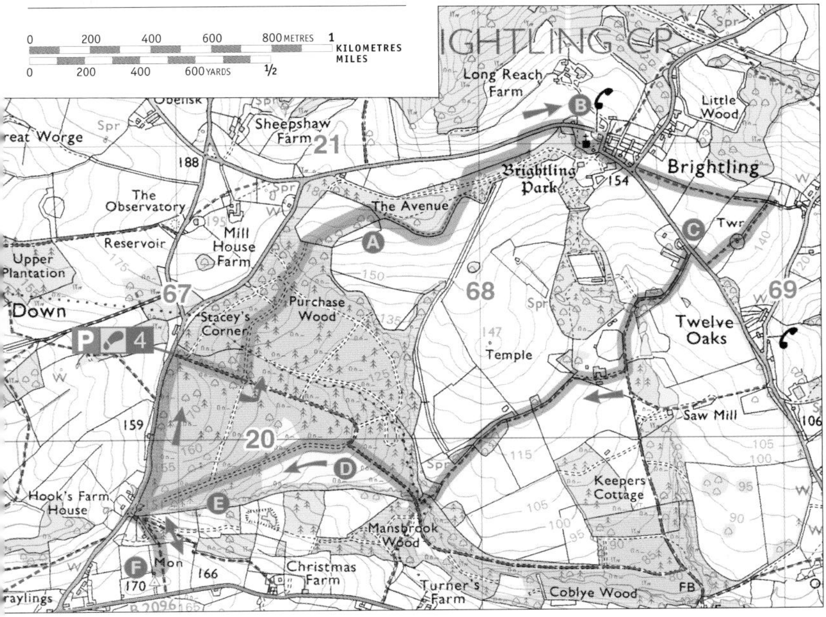

SCALE 1:25000 or 2½ INCHES to 1 MILE 4CM to 1KM

Barcombe Mills and the Ouse Valley

Start	Barcombe Mills
Distance	4½ miles (7.2km)
Height gain	Negligible
Approximate time	2 hours
Parking	Car park at Barcombe Mills
Route terrain	Old railway track, field and riverside paths
Ordnance Survey maps	Landranger 198 (Brighton & Lewes), Explorer OL11 (Brighton & Hove)

GPS waypoints

Start	TQ 433 146
A	TQ 440 160
B	TQ 444 173
C	TQ 442 160
D	TQ 439 152

Perfect for a summer's evening, this short, easy ramble explores the peaceful Ouse Valley, following a former railway track before returning through lush water meadows beside the meandering River Ouse to Barcombe Mills, a scenic riverside spot where the Ouse tumbles over weirs. The Anchor Inn provides the ideal riverside pit stop just over the halfway point.

Although mentioned in Domesday records and locally famed for its cluster of mills and attractive weirs, Barcombe Mills was relatively unknown until the railway came in 1858. It then expanded into a thriving industrious population whose numbers were increased by day trippers brought by the railway. The mills provided employment to local people over the centuries in a number of guises, from flour mill to a button factory. The last mill burned down in 1939 and, with the closure of the railway in 1969, the hamlet is once again rarely visited.

Take the narrow path to the left of the car park entrance to join a tarmac track that soon joins the Sussex Ouse Valley Way, crossing a series of bridges over streams and the River Ouse. Note the toll charges on the former tollgate, the first in Sussex dating from 1066, beside the last bridge stating carriage and horse 1s, steam engines 2s, among others. At a junction by driveways, turn left and soon walk past a line of cottages to reach the road. Continue ahead for a few paces and take the track on the right, signed Anchor Lane 1 mile, opposite the ticket office at the former railway station.

Although the last train chugged along the Wealden Line between Lewes and Uckfield on 23 February 1969, evidence of this once popular rural line remains. The old station at Barcombe Mills, now a private house, was converted and restored retaining many of the original Victorian features in 1985. Farther up the line, Isfield Station was sold in 1983 and following extensive refurbishment it became the centrepiece of the Lavender Line, a heritage railway that operates steam

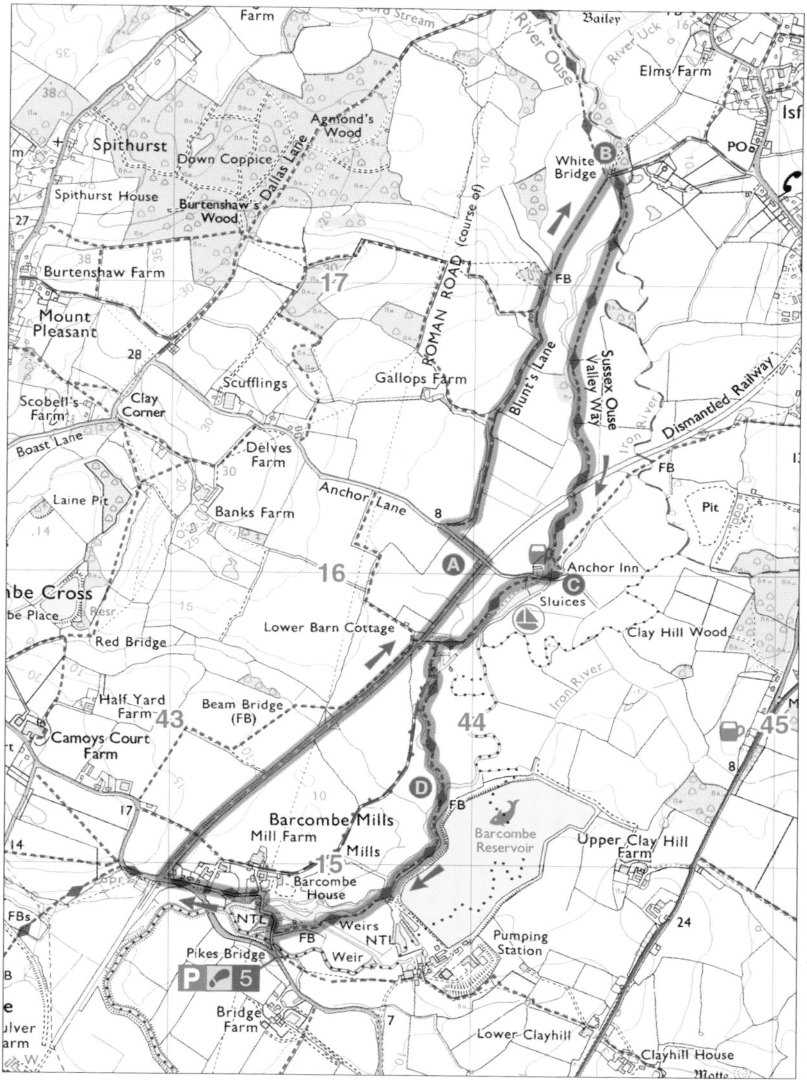

SCALE 1:25 000 or 2½ INCHES to 1 MILE 4CM to 1KM

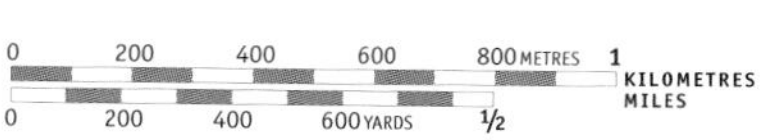

train rides along a mile (1.6km) of preserved track north of the village.

The first section of the bridleway along the former track bed can be very muddy in winter as it is used as a farm track, the going underfoot becoming easier beyond. Cross a stream, then where the track curves left into a field, keep ahead beside a bungalow, the narrow hedged bridleway leading to Anchor Lane **A**.

Turn left for 200 yards and turn right through a gate. Keep left along the field edge, the bridleway soon becoming a wide grassy and hedged track between fields. Ignore the footpath away to your left as the track widens to a clearing and continue along what is known as Blunt's Lane on the map to a gate. Pass beside the wartime pillbox ahead, walk along a line of trees and soon locate a stile by a gate in a group of trees in the field corner. Drop down and bear left beside a stream and cross the footbridge ahead. Bear diagonally left across the meadow, making for and going through the gate ahead to cross the bridge over the River Ouse B.

Climb the stile on the other side to join the Sussex Ouse Valley Way and head south beside the river through water meadows, with views towards the distant South Downs. Eventually pass beneath the old railway and keep to the riverside path to reach the **Anchor Inn** visible ahead. Go through a gate C, cross the footbridge over the river and bear left in front of the pub to reach a gate to the right of sluice gates.

Pass another pillbox, bear right in front of a white-painted house to a gate, then on reaching a drive, bear right to locate a footbridge beyond a barn. Cross the bridge, turn immediately left and continue beside the river to eventually reach a footbridge close to Barcombe Reservoir D.

Walk between the river and high banks of the reservoir to a gate and continue to a footbridge. Follow the path right to climb steps onto a tarmac track by one of the bridges at Barcombe Mills. Turn left back to the car park. ●

Across the River Ouse to the Anchor Inn at Barcombe

Pevensey Levels

Start	Pevensey
Distance	5 miles (8km)
Height gain	Negligible
Approximate time	2 hours
Parking	Pay and Display car park by Pevensey Castle and Tearoom
Route terrain	Field and riverside paths
Ordnance Survey maps	Landranger 199 (Eastbourne & Hastings), Explorers OL25 (Eastbourne & Beachy Head) and 124 (Hastings & Bexhill)

GPS waypoints

- Start: TQ 646 048
- A: TQ 638 047
- B: TQ 639 058
- C: TQ 626 068
- D: TQ 630 067
- E: TQ 637 063
- F: TQ 642 054

The meadowlands of the Pevensey Levels may be flat but they are seldom tedious, especially to the naturalist or ornithologist. These pastures are lonely and the landscape is dominated by the mood of the sky. This route explores footpaths and bridleways that lead through countryside largely neglected by walkers, and it is interesting to speculate on how the landscape appeared some 2,000 years ago when the Romans made Pevensey a fortified gateway into Britain. One thousand years later Saxon outlaws probably used the marshlands to escape from the Norman overlords. Great care should be taken when crossing the busy A27 between waypoints A and B, and on the return after F.

Walk to the bottom end of the car park and go through the gate into the recreation ground. Follow the path round to the right, below the ramparts of the castle. When the original castle was built by the Romans this land would have been under water, as it was in Norman times when the Roman sea fort was enlarged by Robert, Count of Mortain, into a substantial stronghold. Although often besieged it was never taken, and its defence works proved useful in the Second World War when machine gun redoubts were concealed in the walls as an answer to the threat of German invasion.

The sea once lapped against the walls of the eastern and southern perimeter of the castle, and the footpath skirts these by pretty meadows to reach the churchyard of St Mary's, Westham. The Normans set about building the church here at the same time as they started on the neighbouring castle. The church tower is squat yet powerful, a symbol of strength which, though not tall, is a distinctive landmark.

Turn left out of the churchyard onto the main road and then right into Peelings Lane, passing the village hall. Bear right when the road forks by the end of the pond. Turn right again at Castle Farm A, climb a stile leading out of the farmyard, and head straight on over the brow of the low rise in the meadow ahead towards the bypass. Climb a stile and keep ahead, crossing a footbridge and another stile to reach the road.

After crossing carefully, climb a stile and head directly across the meadow towards an observatory seen on the horizon – the route is well-waymarked – going through a gate and over a stile to reach a footbridge and waymarked post B. At the post, do not cross the bridge but take the bridleway left along the south bank of Pevensey Haven. It is little use looking for breakwaters and quays here, since the river has long been closed for navigation. Instead, you may see herons or kingfishers hunting its peaceful waters.

The bridleway continues, close by the bank of the placid waterway, until a tall pylon ahead heralds the end of this pleasant section. The path skirts the left side of the farmyard at Bridge Farm to reach a quiet country lane C. Turn right and then immediately right again onto the road to Pevensey that crosses the river, which is now known as the Yotham. Continue down the road for nearly 1/4 mile (400m), passing beneath electricity cables and following the road as it bends left at a gate giving access to an angling club, and then left again. At this second corner D cross a stile on the right at a footpath sign.

From here the tower of Pevensey church can be seen to the south-east and this landmark is a useful guide on the next section of the walk, over water

The remains of the Norman castle of Pevensey

meadows to Chilley Green.

After crossing the stile walk a few paces to the left, climb another stile and bear left around the edge of the meadow. There is a stile and footbridge by a clump of bushes on the far side. After crossing the bridge turn right to walk along the field edge beside a ditch. This will eventually bring you to a gate. Pass through this to another gate ahead, then keep left beside the hedge and follow a short track to the road at Chilley Green Ⓔ. Turn right and then right again, immediately after the farm, onto a track which leads to Chilley Farm Shop. Pass in front of the shop and beside a pond, then go through a gate on the left just beyond the farmyard. Cross the field to a footbridge and continue directly across the next two fields, heading once more for the tower of Pevensey church.

This leads to the banks of Pevensey Haven again and to a long footbridge. Cross the bridge Ⓑ and turn left, following the bridleway along the waterside until a blue waymark on a post Ⓕ directs you to a metal gate, from where a path leads, with a couple of twists, to the bypass. Cross carefully again, go through a gate and walk along an enclosed path which emerges onto a road in Pevensey in front of the castle walls. Turn left to return to the starting point. ●

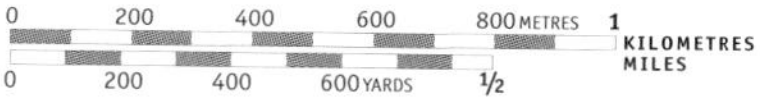

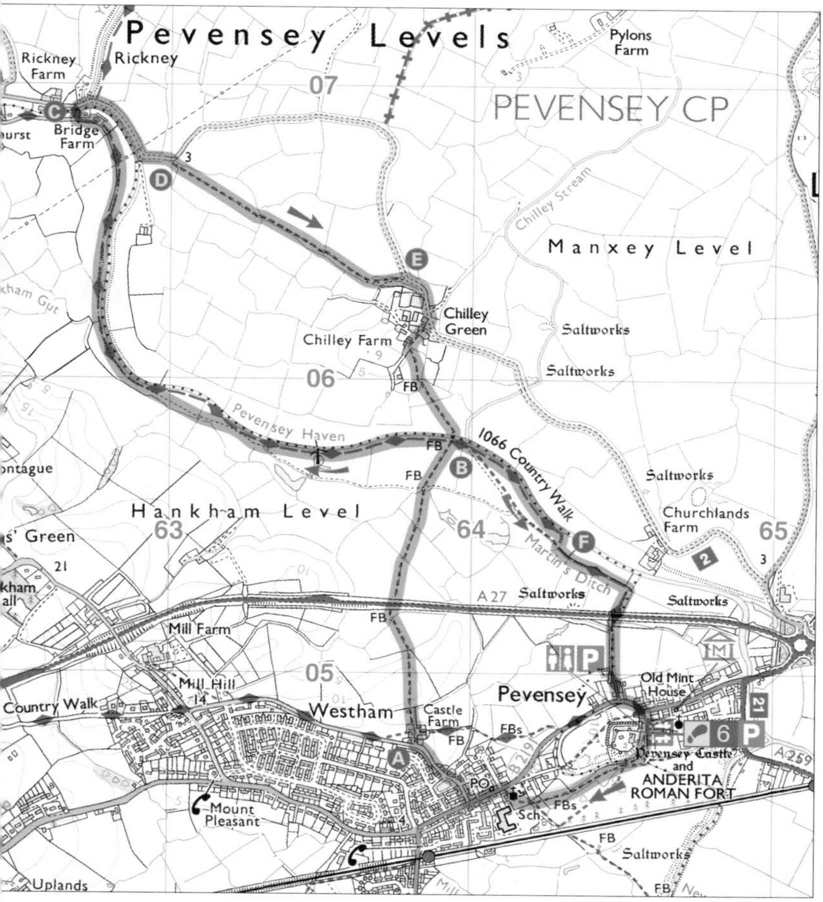

SCALE 1:25 000 or 2½ INCHES to 1 MILE *4CM to 1KM*

Cuckmere Haven from Seaford

Start	Seaford
Distance	4½ miles (7.2km)
Height gain	510 feet (155m)
Approximate time	2½ hours
Parking	Roadside parking and car parks close to the Martello Tower Museum on the seafront
Route terrain	Downland and town streets
Ordnance Survey maps	Landrangers 198 (Brighton & Lewes) and 199 (Eastbourne & Hastings), Explorer OL25 (Eastbourne & Beachy Head)

GPS waypoints

Start	TV 484 985
A	TV 487 982
B	TV 509 973
C	TV 513 976
D	TV 504 980
E	TV 498 981

There is a climb at the start of this walk but this is steep for only a short way. The summit comes at 282 feet (86m) on Seaford Head, where the wonderful coastline of the Seven Sisters is revealed in the distance. The way back is along the northern edge of a nature reserve. Birdwatchers and botanists will appreciate varied habitats that attract many unusual species.

Walk eastwards along the seafront from the Martello Tower, which houses a local history museum with displays illustrating the ways of life of previous generations who lived in Seaford. It also offers the opportunity of seeing the interior of one of the forts built against the threat of Napoleonic invasion. This is Tower No. 74, the westernmost of the 103 that begin at Aldeburgh, in Suffolk, and end here. There is a good view of the chalky ledges of Seaford Head as you approach the beginning of the cliff path **A**. The cliffs here are home to a colony of kittiwakes that come to breed each year (February/March – August).

At the sign for the long-distance Vanguard Way head up the path (or steps) keeping fencing on the right, and continue up the grassy slope, which becomes steeper further up, to reach the top of Seaford Head. The effort is quite

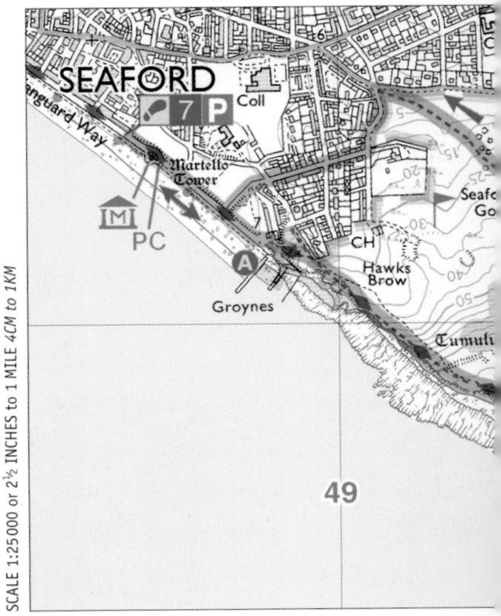

strenuous but the views and sense of space improve with every step. Look back at the town when you take a breather. It was a thriving port until 1573, when a storm threw up a shingle ridge and diverted the River Ouse northwards. Its fortunes revived in the 19th century when the railway arrived and several large hotels were built. The last of these establishments closed many years ago.

From Seaford Head the wonderful Seven Sisters can be seen in the distance. Haven Brow is the nearest and highest of the cliffs at 253 feet (77m). The cliff face of Beachy Head (534 feet/163m high and not one of the Sisters) is hidden from view on the other side of Birling Gap. The profile of the Sisters, with their plunging slopes, illustrates a feature of the geology of chalk country: dry valleys, here seen in section.

The Seaford Head Nature Reserve covers 370 acres (150ha) of chalk grassland, saltmarsh and shingle. Fulmars can be seen soaring with the help of the updraft from the cliffs. In the autumn, the gaps at Short Cliff and Cuckmere Haven attract migrating birds like blackcaps and redstarts.

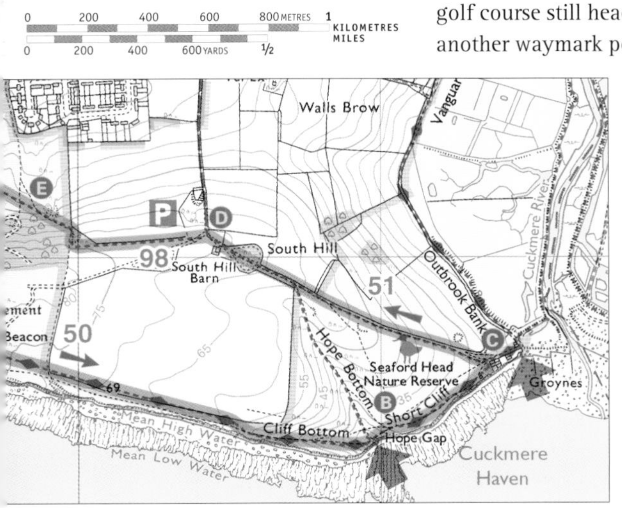

The path descends to Hope Gap **B**, where there is access to the shoreline with its rock pools. Climb the other side of Short Cliff. The chimneys of the cottages at Cuckmere Haven – the foreground of countless photographs – come into view. The Haven was once a famous venue with smugglers and remains isolated from public roads.

Turn left onto the drive from the cottages **C**. The view inland is outstanding as you climb South Hill. Pass South Hill Barn and bear left through a car park **D**. Just before the barrier and concrete drive fork right across the grass through a gap in the hedge and follow the path along the right-hand field edge beside a hedge. The outskirts of Seaford sprawl below to the right.

Follow the waymark right after an enclosed section of path and descend to emerge on open downland. Ignore the first path forking left between bushes and just after it take the left fork **E**, heading north-west. Keep ahead at a crossing path and continue past a waymark post and vegetation on the right. Bear right at a fork and follow the path between bushes, pass a golf ball warning sign and carry on across the golf course still heading north-west to another waymark post and warning sign. Maintain direction, the path ending at the intersection of Chyngton Road and Southdown Road. Turn left onto the latter and then right into Corsica Road which takes you back to the seafront via Cliff Gardens. ●

Burwash and Bateman's

Start	Burwash
Distance	5 miles (8km)
Height gain	525 feet (160m)
Approximate time	2½ hours
Parking	Car park next to the Bear Inn
Route terrain	Field and woodland paths
Ordnance Survey maps	Landranger 199 (Eastbourne & Hastings), Explorer 136 (High Weald, Royal Tunbridge Wells)

GPS waypoints

- TQ 673 246
- Ⓐ TQ 668 251
- Ⓑ TQ 663 254
- Ⓒ TQ 652 236
- Ⓓ TQ 657 232
- Ⓔ TQ 671 238

This walk features views over unspoilt countryside, and much of the return half is over National Trust land surrounding Rudyard Kipling's former home, Bateman's. Allow time to visit the house and enjoy some refreshment in the excellent tearoom.

Burwash is a most attractive village with handsome houses and a church that retains its Norman tower.

Turn right out of the car park adjacent to the **Bear Inn** onto the village street and then left just after the post office down the lane leading to the **Rose and Crown** pub. Take the track (Ham Lane) to the left of the playing field. After ½ mile (800m), turn left through a gate and follow an arrow across the meadow, descending to a stile beyond barns into woodland. The clearly defined path winds through trees to another stile and meadow. Bear right to a stile in the bottom left corner of this field, but do not climb this. Instead turn left to follow the stream and reach a gate in the corner of the field. Walk down the long, narrow meadow that follows and go through another iron gate at the end of this, on the right Ⓐ. Cross the stream and climb towards Mottynsden Farm, making for the iron gate to the right of the oast house. Go through this and pass between the farmhouse and the manor to find a driveway leading right towards a modern house. Where the driveway curves right, continue ahead on a path that ascends the bank, to a stile and enters an orchard. Turn right uphill along the edge of the orchard and go through a gate at the top of the orchard Ⓑ, which leads to a metalled farm track. Turn left, passing a plaque to Flight Lieutenant R.F. Rimmer, killed in action here during the Battle of Britain.

When the track meets a lane, turn left and pass Holton Farm before turning right onto a track at the side of the farm. Glimpses of open countryside are the foretaste of a splendid panorama of pastoral landscape which will be enjoyed at the top of the hill. After this, the path descends gently through woodland to reach Woodlands Farm.

The bridleway passes to the right of the farm, and soon becomes a sunken track. This climbs and becomes narrow and overgrown. When the bridleway meets a farm track, bear left, but leave this before the top of the hill by turning left Ⓒ to follow a further section of ancient enclosed trackway, to reach the A265 opposite Weald House and the Burwash Weald village sign.

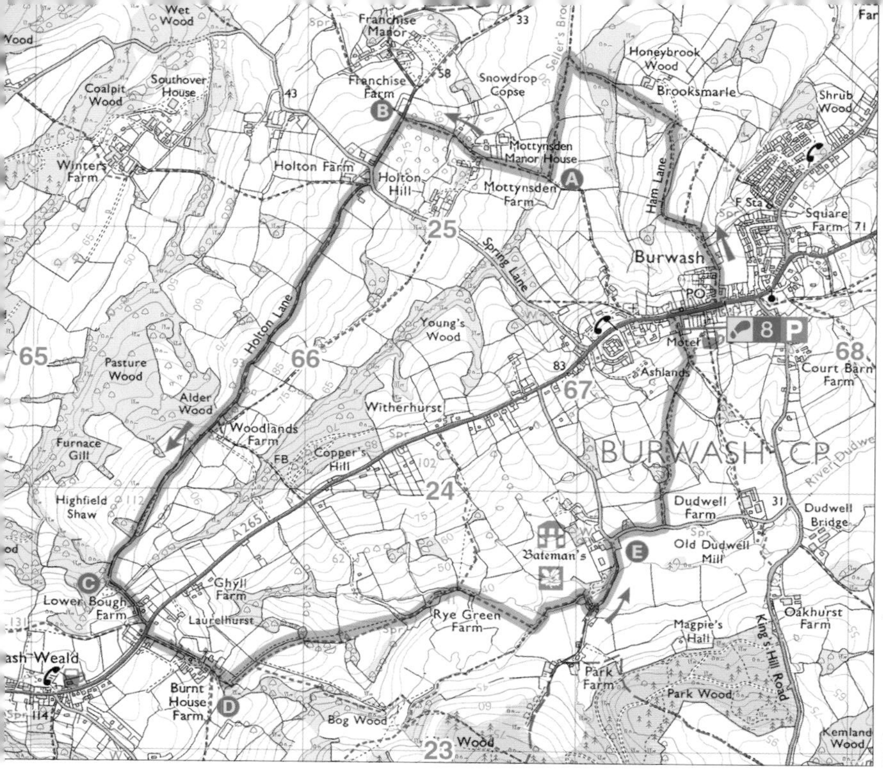

SCALE 1:27777 or about 2¼ INCHES to 1 MILE *3.6CM to 1KM*

0 200 400 600 800 METRES 1 KILOMETRES
0 200 400 600 YARDS ½ MILES

Turn right and walk a short distance along the main road, turning left just beyond Weald House, past concrete posts, to join the drive to Burnt House Farm. Keep straight on at the end of the drive to pass between the houses (the one on the right incorporates oast houses), making for a metal gate leading into a paddock. Go through the gate and pass through a kissing-gate on the left to descend to another gateway. Pass through the gateway **D** and turn left, following the yellow arrow and a fence. Keep to the right of this fence to a gate, pass through and continue along the fence until it ends at a gateway. Drop down across the next field to a stile and then walk through a few trees, passing a pond on the right, to cross another field. Halfway across, Bateman's comes into view ahead.

The path emerges onto an asphalted drive that becomes a farm track as it heads towards a barn. The track ends at a gate and stile, where you bear right, and walk for a short distance, keeping the hedge on the right, to reach another stile. Turn right to cross the stream and then bear left to cross the next, large field, making for the iron railings of a bridge in the fringe of trees on the far side. Cross the bridge, turn left and follow the path to a beautiful mill-pond, where it reaches a lane, and turn left.

The lane passes the north front of Bateman's, a fine 17th-century building. where Rudyard Kipling lived. At the front of the house, turn right **E** and after about 300 yards look for a stile on the left. Go over this and follow a line of old oaks to the right. Skirt the right side of a wood and from its corner go across the meadow to a stile on the far side. From here the path climbs towards Burwash, following the left-hand field edge to a plank bridge by an oak tree. After this bear left uphill and keep the fence on the left until a stile is reached. Cross this to a short path back to the car park. ●

Firle Beacon and Charleston Farmhouse

Start	Firle
Distance	5 miles (8km)
Height gain	740 feet (225m)
Approximate time	2½ hours
Parking	Village car park behind The Ram Inn
Route terrain	Downland and field paths
Ordnance Survey maps	Landrangers 198 (Brighton & Lewes) and 199 (Eastbourne & Hastings), Explorer OL25 (Eastbourne & Beachy Head)

GPS waypoints

- Start: TQ 469 074
- A: TQ 481 059
- B: TQ 490 054
- C: TQ 490 069
- D: TQ 479 070

From Firle, a timeless feudal estate village surrounding the Gage family mansion, this short walk climbs to Firle Beacon on the South Downs Way for wonderful Wealden and sea views, returning along the base of the Downs to pass Charleston Farmhouse.

Sleepy Firle stands tucked away amid a patchwork of fields and hedgerows below the South Downs escarpment and is a perfect example of what landscape historians call a 'closed village', a rare surviving estate village with a tangible feudal atmosphere.

(Start) Go through the white gate in the wall at the far end of the car park behind the **Ram Inn** and turn right along the track. At the lane by the pub, continue ahead along the village street, passing the village stores and St Peter's Church. In the churchyard you will see the graves of the Bloombury artists Vanessa Bell, her son Quentin Bell and Duncan Grant, who lived at Charleston Farmhouse. Where the tarmac ends at a junction of tracks, by the entrance to Place Farm, follow the wide track ahead, which soon curves left beside a flint wall. Gently climb to a copse, with the South Downs looming away to your right.

At a junction of paths in the trees, turn right and follow the hedged bridleway towards the Downs. Skirt Firle Plantation to reach a gate, and then begin the steep climb to the top of the South Downs, following the chalky path as it sweeps left, up and across the scarp slope. Cresting the top of the slope, pause to savour the rolling downland views south towards Newhaven and the glistening sea beyond, and the stunning panorama north across the Weald to Leith Hill in Surrey on the horizon.

Keep to the path, heading east, soon merging with the South Downs Way (A), a 100-mile (160km) long distance path that follows the length of this impressive downland ridge between Eastbourne and Winchester. Pass the triangulation pillar on top of Firle Beacon and continue along the South Downs Way until you reach an arrowed marker post on your left, which marks the point where a

track descends off the Downs B.

Take this track, go through a gate and begin the steep descent down the scarp slope, the wide grassy path curving left down to a gate at the bottom. Once through the gate, the bridleway continues gently downhill to a crossing of tracks, where you keep straight on to reach Tilton Farm. At the farm buildings, bear left along the concrete drive and follow it right to a junction with the driveway to Charleston Farmhouse. Turn left along the drive to the farmhouse C. Charleston was the bohemian country retreat of the Bloomsbury group of post-Victorian artists, writers and intellectuals, including Vanessa Bell and Duncan Grant, who set up home here in 1916. It has been restored and preserved by the Charleston Trust and a rewarding visit will reveal some fine examples of colourful murals and painted furniture.

Keep to the track between the house, **tearoom** and offices to reach a gate. Go through the gate and the one beyond next to farm buildings (can be muddy), and keep left along the hedge through a narrow field to a gate in the field corner. Keep right in the next field, cross a ditch and bear half left to a gate. Climb through the centre of a field on a defined path, passing below Firle Tower away to your right. It was built in 1822 by Viscount Gage to house his head gamekeeper. Cross the drive D to the folly and keep right along the edge of the next field, soon to bear off left along a path that cuts across the field corner. Continue downhill beside a wall towards a cottage and bear right to reach a gate beside the cottage. Exit the drive, cross a track and go through a gate to enter Firle Park.

Follow the arrowed post across the parkland, passing in front of Firle Place, a fine Palladian mansion and home to the Gage family for over 500 years, and cross the tarmac drive to a reach a gate. Follow the track past cottages to reach the village street, turning right by Firle Stores back to the Ram Inn and car park. ●

Bewl Water from Wadhurst

Start	Wadhurst
Distance	5½ miles (8.8km)
Height gain	590 feet (180m)
Approximate time	3 hours
Parking	Either of public car parks in the village, one with its entrance by the White Hart, the other next to the Greyhound
Route terrain	Field and woodland paths
Ordnance Survey maps	Landranger 188 (Maidstone & Royal Tunbridge Wells) and 199 (Eastbourne & Hastings), Explorer 136 (High Weald, Royal Tunbridge Wells)

GPS waypoints

Start	TQ 641 317
A	TQ 644 319
B	TQ 654 324
C	TQ 664 324
D	TQ 665 326
E	TQ 669 329
F	TQ 662 318
G	TQ 656 313

Bewl Water is the largest area of open water in the south of England – there is a 13-mile (21km) walk around its perimeter. This walk takes in part of its less-frequented southern shore. Be sure to wear waterproof footwear as the approach path is often wet. It is not advisable to wear shorts on this route.

Wadhurst is one of those places that seems unable to decide whether it is a village or a town (having been granted a charter and a market by Henry III in 1253 it could well claim to be a town). Iron-smelting from local ironstone was probably established when the Romans first came here. In the 17th and 18th centuries Wadhurst prospered from ironfounding – look inside the church to see 31 memorials of cast iron set into the floor. The spire of the church is 128 feet (39m) high and, as this walk shows, is a distinctive landmark.

(Start) Walk down Blacksmith's Lane, opposite the **Greyhound** inn and, when it turns sharply left (A), keep ahead on the drive to Little Pell Farm. Go through the farmyard and join a track with a hedge to the left that descends to a wood and a muddy pond. Bewl Water can be seen ahead.

The reservoir came into operation in 1975 and holds 31,300 million litres of water. It has become famous for its recreational facilities, catering for fly-fishers, windsurfers, yachtsmen and canoeists as well as walkers and cyclists.

The footpath continues through woodland and between fields, eventually reaching a stile and a field. Continue ahead to cross another stile and turn right immediately beyond it at a junction with a bridleway (B). Although this right of way closely follows the shore of the reservoir, there are, as yet, only glimpses of it. Cyclists also use this path and may approach quickly and silently from the rear. After some distance of skirting muddy creeks, the bridleway bursts out into open countryside and a great expanse of Bewl Water is revealed.

Continue along the shore path – if you look back you will see the spire of Wadhurst church rising above the trees.

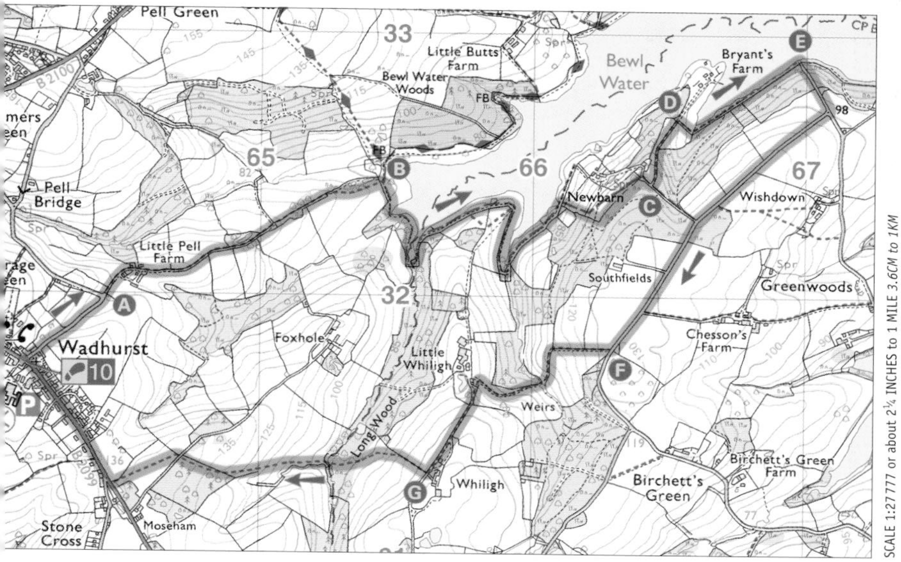

Just beyond a small fisherman's hut, turn right onto a bridleway. At the end of the 18th century this isolated district was famous for its enormous oak trees, among the last remaining from the forest that once covered the Weald. They provided timber for the fighting-ships that sailed under Nelson's command during the wars against France. The difficulties in removing the trees to the dockyards at Chatham and Portsmouth can only be imagined.

The path leaves the shore to skirt the wood behind the farm and oasthouse at Newbarn. Turn right at a lane and, after 50 yards, take the concrete drive on the left **C** that leads towards Bryant's Farm. At the gateway to the farm, take the footpath to the right **D** down some steps and through woodland. There is a nicely sited seat and another fisherman's hut overlooking Bewl Water and a series of fish tanks used for rearing some of the 50,000 trout that are needed each year to restock the lake.

Turn right **E** onto the lane that (in the other direction) disappears beneath the water of the reservoir. Go right again at the road junction at the top of the hill and walk along the quiet lane

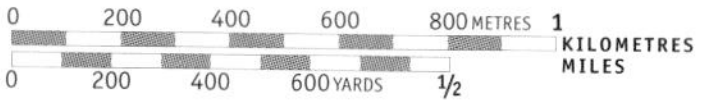

for almost a mile (1.6km), climbing at first. Pass the lane to Chesson's Farm on the left. Less than 1/4 mile (400m) farther on where the lane begins to bend left, take the footpath on the right **F** that follows a hedge to the bottom of the field. Turn left after passing two fine oaks to go through a gate and across a bridge. A track takes the route to Little Whiligh. Turn left along the drive to see Wadhurst church on the skyline again.

When a drive rises on the left to Whiligh stableyard, descend the steps on the right **G** and go through a kissing-gate. The path follows the hedge down at first but veers left after a hawthorn tree towards a stile in the fence at the bottom. Bear left along a grassy path to a gate and a bridge over a stream of reddish water.

Walk up the edge of a large field with fence, trees and hedge on the left. In the top corner exit to a lane, cross over and go diagonally across this pasture to reach the B2099 at Stone Cross. Turn right here and follow the pavement into Wadhurst.

Herstmonceux

Start	Herstmonceux
Distance	5½ miles (8.9km)
Height gain	560 feet (170m)
Approximate time	3 hours
Parking	Car park in village centre
Route terrain	Field and woodland paths
Ordnance Survey maps	Landranger 199 (Eastbourne & Hastings), Explorer 124 (Hastings & Bexhill)

GPS waypoints

- Start: TQ 634 125
- A TQ 636 124
- B TQ 632 117
- C TQ 635 113
- D TQ 639 114
- E TQ 643 111
- F TQ 643 101
- G TQ 653 103
- H TQ 647 110
- J TQ 645 118

This country walk gives a good view of Herstmonceux Castle, a romantic building dating from 1441 with its towers and turrets reflected in the waters of its moat. The walk covers farmland and woodland in a beautiful part of East Sussex but some of the paths have been neglected and are unmarked, so careful map reading is important.

The parish church and the famous castle are two miles (3.2km) distant from the centre of Herstmonceux both by road and by footpath. The village is famous for its trugs, garden baskets skilfully made of wood, invented here by Thomas Smith, who took samples to London in 1851 and showed them to Queen Victoria at Buckingham Palace. The Trug Shop bearing his name is to be found in Hailsham Road.

From the car park by the Health Centre in the middle of the village, walk to the main road and cross from the **Woolpack Inn** to take the footpath by the Gardener Street nameboard. The asphalted path climbs on the edge of the playing field. Go through the kissing-gate at the top A and bear right towards a lone oak tree. Pass this to reach a kissing-gate in the corner of the field.

Walk with the fence to the left, facing a wonderful view across the Pevensey Levels to the sea and downs. Bear slightly right at the end of the fence to a metal gate on the far side of the field. Go through here – and the second gate a few paces farther on – and continue across the next field to a kissing-gate. Bear gently left to cross another field to a second kissing-gate. Turn left and then almost immediately right B and turn left before a metal gate to cross a meadow with another overgrown pond to the left. The discernible path across the meadow takes you to a gap in the hedge. Bear left across the next meadow, heading to the right of a house and drop down to cross a footbridge and stile. Now make for the left side of the garden ahead and cross two stiles before reaching a lane at Butler's Farmhouse.

Cross to the footpath opposite and follow the left-hand edge of a field to a gateway C. The right of way crosses the next field diagonally, heading to the left of the house on the far side. Turn right after a stile to reach the road past a barn and cottage (Little Butlers). Turn left and, after 50 yards take the enclosed path on the right to a gate, descending the field edge to a footbridge **D**. However, do not cross this but, 10 yards before it, go through the small metal gate to the right and cross the footbridge and the track ahead. Follow the field edge as it curves left beside a drainage ditch. Continue through the gate and, 20 yards farther on, go through a metal field gate, then follow the track uphill to a gateway visible on the skyline. Look to the right for a fine view of Herstmonceux Place with its classical façade. At the top **E** turn right onto a bridleway and walk down by the hedge to the bottom of the dip. Do not follow the track to the right but keep ahead and climb the steep slope to a metal gate by a birch tree. A pleasant stretch of level woodland walking follows. Keep ahead when a footpath crosses and bear left when you reach Church Road.

Pass the church and turn left onto a bridleway **F** that is part of the 1066 Country Walk. This crosses the driveway to the Observatory (Herstmonceux Castle was the headquarters of the Royal Greenwich Observatory for 40 years until it was acquired by Queen's University, Canada, in 1993, which

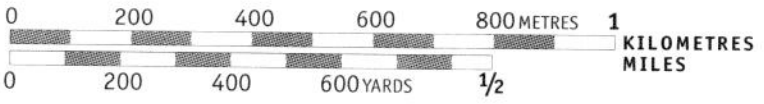

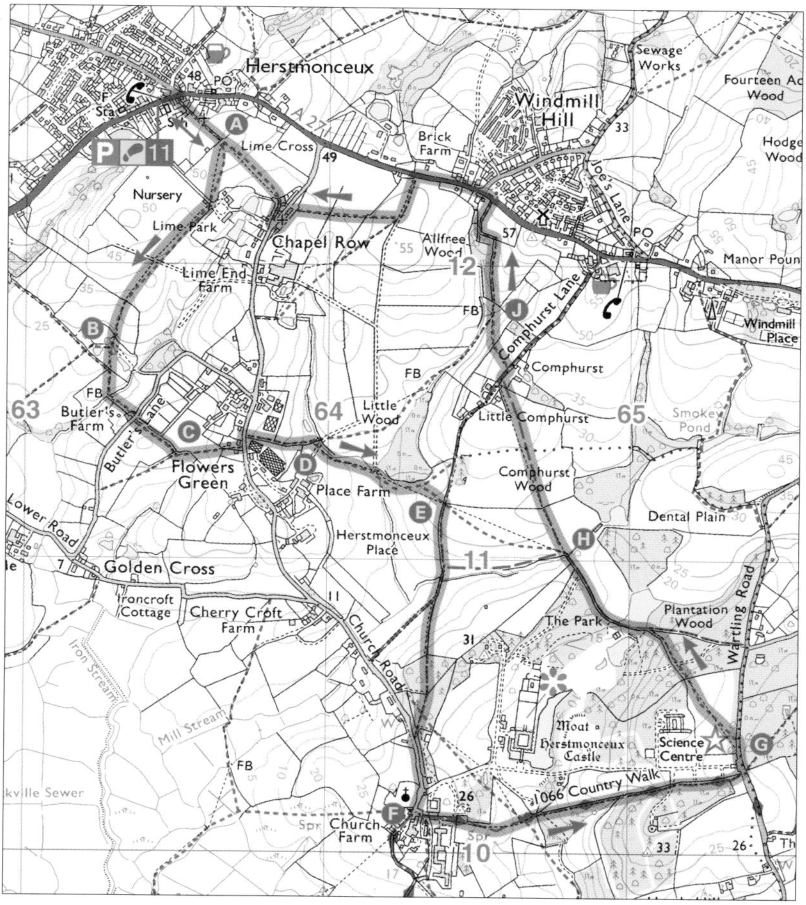

SCALE 1:25 000 or 2½ INCHES to 1 MILE *4CM to 1KM*

Herstmonceux Castle

established the International Study Centre). On the other side of the drive the path soon emerges from woodland to give an excellent view of the south side of the moated castle. Remarkably, much of this is fairly modern – rebuilding took place in 1912. The original interior had been stripped at the end of the 18th century to provide building material for Herstmonceux Place. However, the exterior survives and is notable for being one of the largest castles of its date in the country, and the first to be built of brick.

The pleasant walking continues along the bridleway to reach a road near the drive to the Science Centre. Turn left and, after 100 yards, go left through a gate G and walk diagonally across the field. After a stile in the far corner, the path descends through Plantation Wood and bears left onto a track that passes between the park's two lakes. There is a good view of Herstmonceux Place to the left when this bridleway emerges into open country.

Keep straight on at a path junction H, making for a barn on the skyline. Go through a metal gate, and keep ahead until you reach Comphurst Lane. Turn right, and follow the lane for 100 yards. Cross the stile on the left opposite the entrance to Comphurst itself and follow the footpath across two meadows to reach a stile by Allfree Wood J. The windmill on top of Windmill Hill overlooks this pretty valley. Walk up the east side of the wood to the main road and turn left.

After about 300 yards on the footway, take the footpath on the left and climb for about 160 yards. Now turn right through a small metal gate and make for a point about 50 yards to the right of the chapel, where another small gate brings you to the former Welcome Stranger at Chapel Row. Despite the encouraging notices on the wall, the old pub is no longer open for business.

Turn left; then, opposite the chapel, take the footpath on the right that initially seems to run in the wrong direction. However, it soon swings left to a kissing-gate. The roof of the sports pavilion passed early in the walk can be seen on the skyline beyond a long meadow. Go through a kissing-gate A close to the pavilion to rejoin the path by the side of the recreation ground near the start.

Rye from Iden

Start	Iden church
Distance	6 miles (9.7km)
Height gain	310 feet (95m)
Approximate time	3 hours
Parking	Recreation ground car park at start
Route terrain	Field and riverside paths; town centre
Ordnance Survey maps	Landranger 189 (Ashford & Romney Marsh), Explorer 125 (Romney Marsh, Rye & Winchelsea)

GPS waypoints

- Start: TQ 915 237
- A: TQ 914 232
- B: TQ 911 219
- C: TQ 912 215
- D: TQ 916 208
- E: TQ 925 206
- F: TQ 932 224
- G: TQ 925 235

Parking is at a premium at Rye in the summer but this walk presents a way of overcoming the problem. Although some of the paths on the route seem to be underused, it gives unusual views of the town and the freedom to take time to explore it fully. At times careful map-reading is needed.

There is a small car park at the recreation ground by All Saints' Church at Iden or, if this is full, there is always adequate on-street parking in the village. Iden wins a mention in *The Guinness Book of Records* as the two rectors who held office from 1807 served 117 years between them, the second one dying in 1924. The sturdy, battlemented tower is the main feature of the church, dating from the 11th century.

(Start) Walk past the west end of the church to a group of small oak trees in the corner of the playing field. Here a well-concealed and unwaymarked footpath starts on the left, swinging right to reach a stile. After this it follows the edge of a field with a fence to the left, descending to a plank bridge and stile at the bottom. Follow the waymark to the right and make your way through a 'conservation meadow', planted with uniform lines of fruit trees. Beyond them cross a field, go through a gate and keep left along the field edge to a stile by an asbestos hut.

Cross a bridleway and the stile on the other side **A** and keep ahead to find a metal stile by a beech tree. Turn right to follow a hedge down to the corner of Tighe's Wood. The path is faint as it leads along the edge of the wood and descends to another metal stile at the end of a row of sweet chestnut trees. The path is more obvious as it climbs with a fence to the left to a stile and continue to reach the A268, meeting the road at a weatherboarded cottage.

Turn left for 20 yards and then go right on a grassy bridleway, dropping down into a little valley. Make for the field corner and continue on the path when it becomes enclosed by trees and bushes. Pass a path on the left and soon follow the path right into a field, keeping right into an adjacent field corner **B**. Turn left along the field edge until you see a waymark and swing right across the field, heading uphill towards the boundary.

The steady climb leads you to a gap in the hedge close to the field corner. Keep ahead along a field edge path to a stile and enter the yard of Leasam Farm. Keep ahead past Leasam Byre and, where the drive swings left, leave it to the right **C** to follow a fenced path through woodland. Cross an asphalted driveway to a kissing-gate that gives the first view of Rye with its windmill well seen ahead. There is an even better view from the stile a little way farther down Leasam Hill, at the top of a belt of trees.

Descend to Rolvendene Farm, go through a gate and bear left in front of the farm, then keep right to follow the path along the grassy embankment between the river and the drive. Go right when you reach a surfaced footpath **D** and pass a row of terrace houses before coming to the main road. Turn left to the level crossing and so come to the town centre.

Most people will like to make their own way through Rye with its fascinating old streets and alleys, and equally intriguing and diverse shops and eating places. The route passes through the town from west to east and leaves it by the London road (A259) that crosses the River Rother after a roundabout. Walk along to the road bridge, cross it and then turn left to join the Saxon Shore Way **E**.

The path forms part of the Saxon Shore Way, the Sussex Border Path and the Royal Military Canal footpath. There is little headroom as it goes beneath the railway bridge but after this the walking is enjoyable, with the river and gentle hills to the left and Romney Marsh to the right. Cross the Union Canal and, 1/2 mile (800m) farther on, turn left to cross the river at Scots Float Sluice **F**.

Cross the road to a footbridge on the other side, which forms the start of a path that climbs into a wood, with steps helping the ascent up steep slopes. The stile at the top gives on to a clearly defined path across a large field. Cross the next field diagonally to Houghton Wood. The path goes through the wood, a stream using it in wet weather. After the second of two plank bridges the right of way leaves the trees, crosses the neck of a field and then follows the field edge towards a farmhouse (curiously known as Old Turks).

Go right at the road, then left across a stile onto a waymarked footpath opposite Old Turks **G**. Cross the field diagonally to a stile on the left of a

The approach to Rye

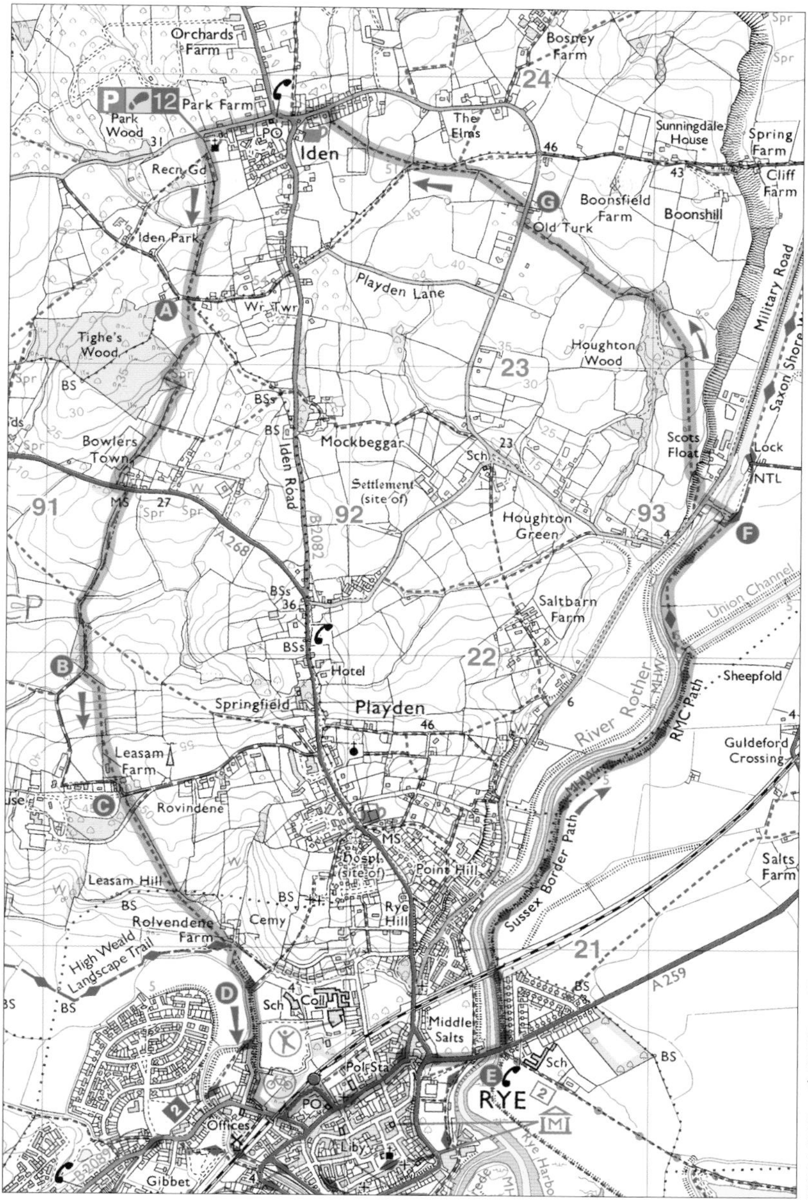

0 200 400 600 800 METRES 1 KILOMETRES
0 200 400 600 YARDS ½ MILES

SCALE 1:25000 or 2½ INCHES to 1 MILE *4CM to 1KM*

metal gate. Keep ahead with a pond to the right, and then follow the boundary hedge, avoiding a waymarked path on the right. Keep to the field edge, then just before reaching a gateway, bear right through a gap in the hedge to follow a path (not waymarked) across the centre of a field to a stile. Continue across the next field to a stile and a narrow path leading to a road. Turn left to a crossroads by **the Bell** and cross over into Church Lane, following it back to the car park.

Hartfield, Withyham and Five Hundred Acre Wood

Start	Hartfield
Distance	6 miles (9.7km)
Height gain	605 feet (185m)
Approximate time	3 hours
Parking	Roadside parking in the village centre
Route terrain	Field and woodland paths; metalled tracks
Ordnance Survey maps	Landranger 188 (Maidstone & Royal Tunbridge Wells), Explorer 135 (Ashdown Forest)

GPS waypoints

Start	TQ 478 359
A	TQ 492 356
B	TQ 490 338
C	TQ 476 335
D	TQ 471 334
E	TQ 474 348
F	TQ 474 352

A.A. Milne, author of the Winnie the Pooh *books, lived near Hartfield, and this part of Ashdown Forest is the setting for many of the stories. The walk takes you through a quiet and undulating part of the forest that lies below the open heathland plateau, an attractive mixture of woodland and pasture with fine views over both the forest and the Weald. It includes two interesting village churches and crosses 'Pooh Bridge', a delightful spot in Posingford Wood where Pooh and his friends indulged in that simple but ever-popular pastime of 'Poohsticks'.*

Hartfield is situated on the edge of Ashdown Forest, an attractive collection of houses and cottages with a fine medieval church dominated by a 15th-century tower and broach spire.

(Start) Walk along Church Street, passing the unusual lychgate to the churchyard on the left. Fifty yards beyond the lychgate, directly opposite the church porch, there is a stile on the right. Climb this and turn left along the edge of the field to another stile by a metal gate. Climb the stile and continue in the same direction to climb a third stile at the far end of the field.

After this the path divides. Take the left fork to cross the field to a point where a line of oak trees – the remnants of an old hedge line – meets the left-hand edge of the field. The waymarked path leads over the next field diagonally, heading for a point to the left of Withyham church. Skirt the right-hand edge of a narrow belt of woodland and continue gently downhill to climb a stile onto a road. Turn right and cross a bridge over a stream. The village with its pub (**Dorset Arms**) is just ahead but the route immediately turns right **A** onto a tarmac drive – signposted for Withyham church – that heads uphill, passing to the right of the church and a large house. Withyham's 14th-century church was largely rebuilt following destruction by lightning in 1663. Inside there are monuments to the Sackville family, earls and dukes of Dorset, formerly the keepers and later the owners of Ashdown Forest.

Continue along the tarmac drive, part of the Wealdway, for the next 1¼ miles (2km), enjoying fine views to the right across the Weald and ahead towards the wooded heights of the forest. Just after passing a row of houses on the right, turn left **B** over a stile in front of a white gate and follow the path beside a wire fence, bearing right and continuing into Five Hundred Acre Wood, the 'One Hundred Acre Wood' of the *Winnie the Pooh* stories. This large area of woodland, an attractive mixture of oak, beech and conifers, was enclosed from the forest in 1693.

Cross a drive on the edge of the wood, keep ahead along another drive, bear right at a T-junction, and at a fork a little way ahead, continue along the right-hand track. At a junction of three tracks take the right-hand one (still following the Wealdway) which curves right and heads downhill following the inside edge of the wood. Bear right at the bottom and continue gently uphill to a fork. Here the Wealdway continues to the left but you keep ahead along the right-hand track, still by the edge of Five Hundred Acre

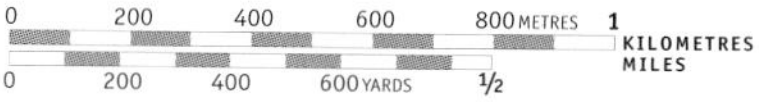

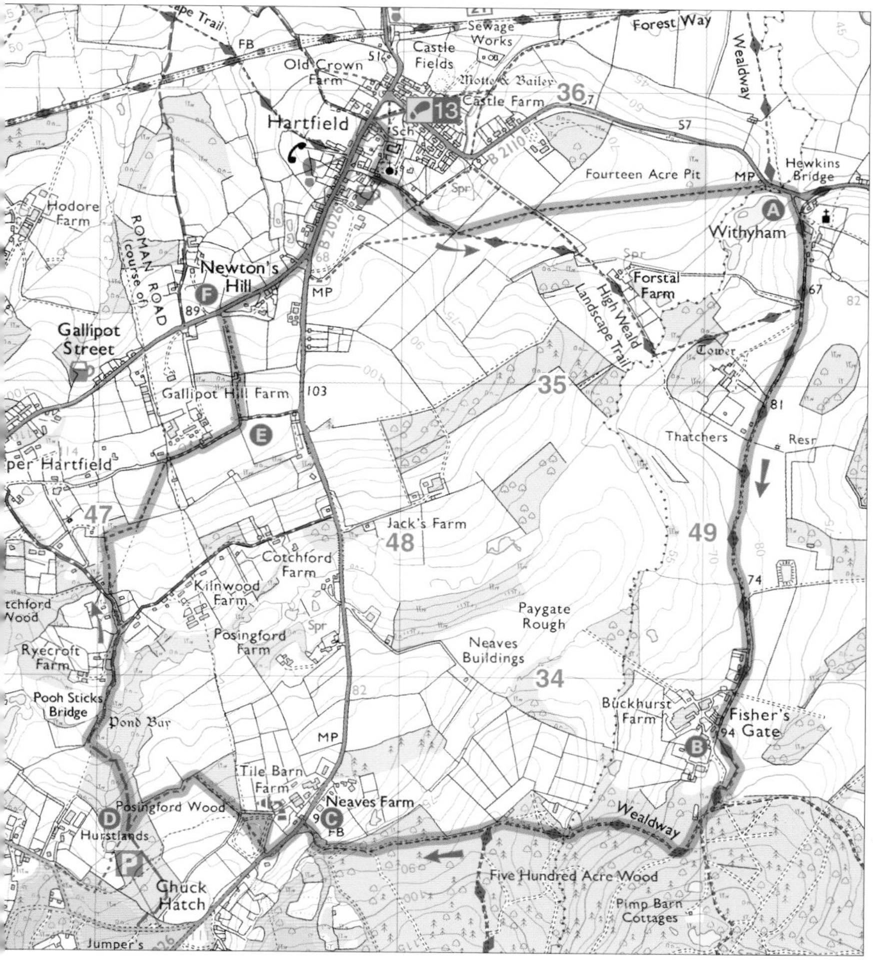

SCALE 1:25 000 or 2½ INCHES to 1 MILE *4CM to 1KM*

Pooh Bridge in Ashdown Forest

Wood, a most attractive part of the walk. Eventually, the track heads uphill between embankments to a road **C**.

Turn left along the road and at a footpath diversion sign and public footpath stone turn right over a stile. *Either follow the footpath arrows across the riding track and exercise area, or turn right and follow the path around the perimeter of a horse exercise area, eventually reaching a stile on the far side.* Climb the stile onto a track at a bend and turn right down the track, soon to take the arrowed path left into a field.

Follow the field edge around to the left and keep ahead to climb a waymarked stile into Posingford Wood. Continue through the wood, go through a gate and then climb a stile on the edge of the trees and bear left. Walk across a field and climb another stile, at a public footpath stone, to re-enter woodland.

About 100 yards ahead meet the surfaced track coming up from the Pooh Car Park (left) **D** and turn right along it, walking beneath the woodland canopy. After passing over a bridge and then bending right the path heads downhill along the edge of woodland to Pooh Bridge where in A.A. Milne's stories, Winnie the Pooh and his friends played 'Poohsticks', dropping sticks into the stream and watching them float under the bridge.

Cross the bridge and continue uphill to join a tarmac drive. Keep ahead and at a public footpath sign turn right over a stile. Walk along the left-hand edge of a field, by a hedge on the left, and follow the field edge round to the right to climb another stile. Continue in the same direction diagonally across the next field, climbing a stile in front of a house. Bear right over the next stile, at a public footpath sign, and bear left to keep along the left-hand edge of a field along an enclosed path. Towards the end of the field turn left through a gate **E** and follow the path ahead across rough grassland, keeping parallel to the edge of woodland on the left. Cross a stile and continue - ahead is a grand view over the Medway Valley and the Weald, with the spire of Hartfield church prominent - eventually crossing a stile onto a road **F**.

Turn right and after 1/4 mile (400m) bear left at a junction into Hartfield. ●

Bodiam Castle and the Rother Valley

Start	Bodiam Castle
Distance	7 miles (11.2km)
Height gain	490 feet (150m)
Approximate time	3½ hours
Parking	Pay and Display National Trust car park
Route terrain	Field and woodland paths
Ordnance Survey maps	Landranger 199 (Eastbourne & Hastings), Explorer 136 (High Weald, Royal Tunbridge Wells)

GPS waypoints

- TQ 783 254
- A TQ 771 254
- B TQ 760 245
- C TQ 750 239
- D TQ 769 238
- E TQ 781 236
- F TQ 787 247

Explore the staircases and battlements and savour the views from Bodiam Castle before setting out on this glorious ramble through the fields, orchards and woodland in the peaceful Rother Valley. If time allows take a steam train trip on the Kent and East Sussex Railway and enjoy lovely Wealden views. Note that Udiam Lane (track) can be wet and muddy in winter.

Bodiam Castle is one of the most famous and evocative castles in Britain. Built in 1385 as both a coastal defence, when the River Rother was then navigable by sea-going vessels, and a comfortable home, the exterior is almost complete and its ramparts rise dramatically above a carp-filled moat.

Leaving the car park, follow the road right and almost immediately turn left between **The Castle** pub and the green to follow a tarmac lane beside the recreation field. Remain on this lane to the Old Cricket Pavilion, where you pass to the right of a gate to join a hedged track. Ignore the next track on the left and beyond it keep left at a fork. Go through a gate and keep ahead along the track passing to the left of a large brick building. At the second building take the arrowed path left across a footbridge **A**.

Pass a pond to locate a narrow path through trees to a stile. Turn right in the field, climb a further stile and bear slightly uphill across the field to a kissing-gate and the B2244. Cross the road (with care) and the stile opposite, turn left uphill and bear right along the line of oak trees to a stile in the field corner. Strike out across the large field ahead, passing to the right of a copse to locate a stile in the line of trees ahead.

Do not cross the stile, instead turn left and walk down the field edge and where it begins to curve left, follow the path right through the trees to cross a footbridge. Bear right through the beech copse to reach a stile and turn left along the field edge to another stile and enter an orchard **B**.

Follow a path arrowed right to Salehurst through the orchard. Follow the arrows right then left and continue through orchards behind Moat Farm, eventually dropping down through trees to a stile by a gate. Walk across two fields and then bear left along a field edge path down to a track. Continue on the track opposite along the right-hand field edge towards Salehurst church. Keep left along the field edge where the track curves right toward a farmhouse and go through a gate into the churchyard. Exit through the lychgate, turn left and then left again by an oak tree (**Salehurst Halt** pub right), and follow the enclosed path (bridleway) that bears right around a house to reach a bridge over the River Rother Ⓒ.

Continue to a metalled drive and turn left, the drive soon bearing right past the entrance gates to a house that incorporates the remains of Robertsbridge Abbey, a Cistercian abbey founded in 1176, and then follow it sharp left to reach a gate. Pass to the left of the gate and stables to locate a stile by a gate. Cross the grass to a further stile to join a fenced path that leads into a field. Walk along the field edge and maintain direction through the next long and narrow field, parallel with the River Rother, the defined grassy path eventually bearing half-right to a gap in the right-hand corner of the field. Continue with

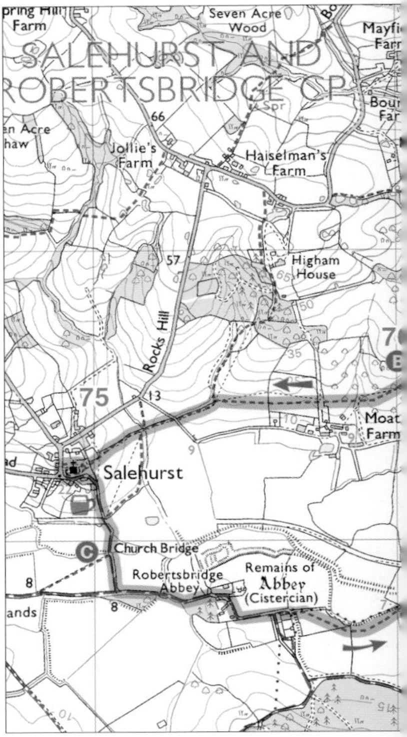

Bodiam Castle

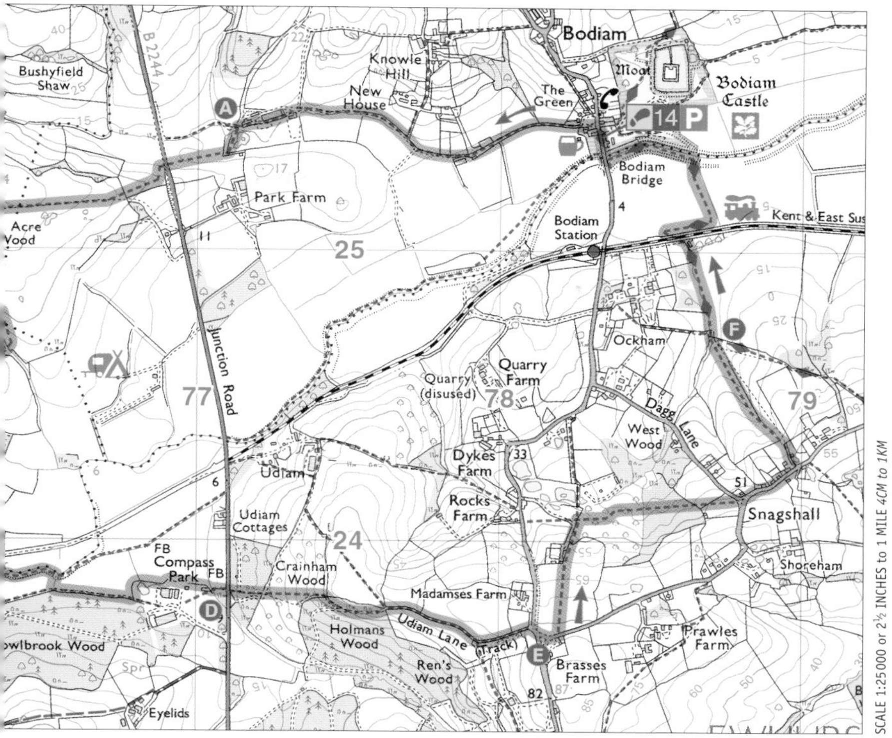

the waymarker along the right-hand field edge towards Compass Park, a modern business estate. On reaching the corner of the field bear round to the left and then right, following the waymarked path round the north side of the park that leads to a footbridge D and, just beyond the trees, the B2244.

Cross the road to the path directly opposite (may be difficult to spot), climb up through Crainham Wood, cross a track and keep ahead through an orchard, bending left along its edge to a stile in the corner. Follow the woodland path right, which soon becomes a sunken track (Udiam Lane) leading to a road. Cross it diagonally to join Shoreham Lane, signed to Ewhurst Green E. In a few paces turn left over a stile, take in the wonderful views north across the Rother Valley, and descend through the field to a gate. Continue along the edge of an old orchard and turn right at a crossing of paths, soon to cross a footbridge and walk through woodland to a stile. Cross the field to a further stile and a road junction.

Follow the road ahead and take the footpath on your left just before Romney Lodge. Cross a stile and head downhill through the field to join the waymarked Sussex Border Path at a junction by a gate F. Go through the gate bearing right to a footbridge by an old corrugated barn and cross the Kent and East Sussex Railway. If you have the time enjoy a 10-mile (16km) steam train ride through the unspoilt Rother Valley to Tenterden. Turn right and walk around the field edge and then beside the river to a gate to the left of Bodiam Bridge. Turn right back to the car park and the National Trust **tearoom**.

Beachy Head and Long Down

Start	Old Lighthouse, 1½ miles (2.4km) west of Beachy Head
Distance	6¾ miles (10.8km)
Height gain	870 feet (265m)
Approximate time	3½ hours
Parking	At start (Pay and Display)
Route terrain	Downland and cliff-edge paths
Ordnance Survey maps	Landranger 199 (Eastbourne & Hastings), Explorer OL25 (Eastbourne & Beachy Head)

GPS waypoints

Start	TV 568 954
A	TV 556 959
B	TV 564 957
C	TV 563 962
D	TV 593 969
E	TV 597 969
F	TV 591 957

After an initial appetiser of clifftop walking around the Old Lighthouse towards Birling Gap, the outward route is on a little-used bridleway that strikes eastwards across Long Down. A famous section of the South Downs Way provides the return, with stunning views of Beachy Head and the Seven Sisters as a climax. Parts of the route may be muddy.

From the car park below the Old Lighthouse, turn westwards and follow the grassy path to the right of the tarmac drive and climb to the lighthouse. Belle Tout was built in the 1830s but its light was often obscured by fog and low cloud. A new lighthouse replaced it in 1902. Belle Tout had a starring role in the popular television adaptation of Fay Weldon's novel *The Life and Loves of a She-Devil*. It was moved back from the edge of the cliff in 1999.

The view back towards the modern lighthouse, beneath Beachy Head, is spectacular. Walk to the other side of the lighthouse and the vista in the opposite direction, over the

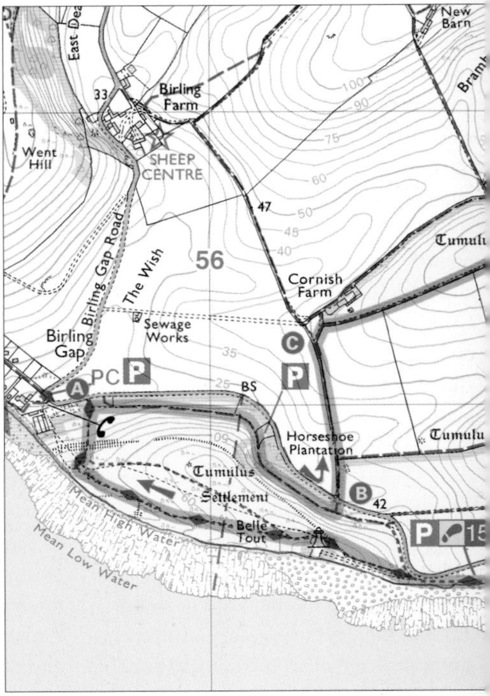

Seven Sisters to Birling Gap and Seaford, is also stunning.

The path descends westwards towards Birling Gap. When the visitor centre (with adjoining shop and **café**) at Birling Gap comes into view, take the grassy path to the right, which almost reaches the road. Bear right to leave the Lookout (a National Trust property) and join a bridleway heading eastwards, parallel to the road **A**. Keep to the right-hand path of the two parallel routes. There is a brief, pleasant spell of woodland walking through Horseshoe Plantation, then take the grassy path left and drop down to the road **B**. Cross it to the concrete track to Cornish Farm.

Ignore a permissive bridleway to the right and continue on the track almost to the farm, turning off through a wooden bridlegate placed by an iron gate **C**. Go through a wooden gate by a paddock and keep fencing on the right as you climb to the crest of Long Down. Pass through several gates and avoid a track on the right to Bullockdown Farm. Keep ahead between fences and stone walls before reaching a gate leading out to the road. Cross it and go forward on a grassy path with the buildings of Eastbourne seen ahead. When you reach a waymark, turn right and follow the Weald Way. Make for the next waymark and turn sharp left towards the seafront **D**. The path descends to give a fine view of the town. At the next seafront sign, turn sharp right to follow the South Downs Way **E**.

The path skirts the top of Whitebread Hole, which must once have been a spectacular landslip. Keep bearing to

0 200 400 600 800 METRES 1 KILOMETRES
0 200 400 600 YARDS 1/2 MILES

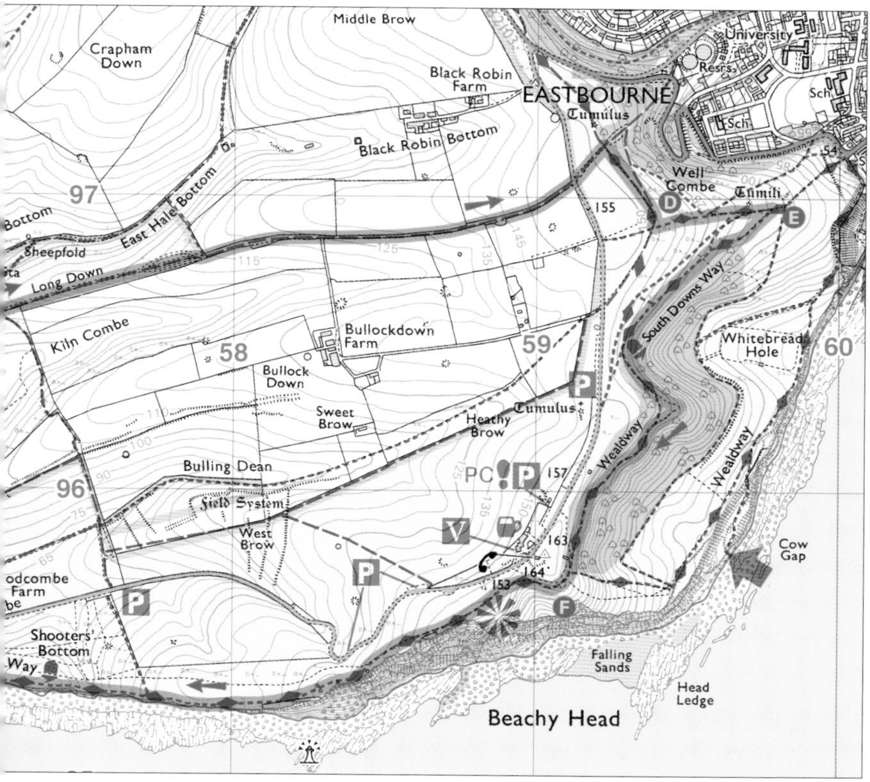

SCALE 1:25000 or 2½ INCHES to 1 MILE *4CM to 1KM*

Beachy Head at dusk

the left around the rim of the Hole, coming close to the road and then swinging away from it. The path becomes asphalted as it approaches Beachy Head Ⓕ. This is necessary because of the crowds who come here by coach and car, few venturing far along the coast path.

The Countryside Centre has interactive displays illustrating the history of this part of the South Downs and how man and beast have been influenced by the unstable geology. Refreshments are available at the **Beachy Head** pub, which has a bar, restaurant and coffee shop.

The lighthouse, 536 feet (163m) below the clifftop, is best seen from near the parking area about 1/4 mile (400m) past the pub, where the road makes a hairpin turn. On a clear day the view extends 40 miles (64km) to the east to Dungeness, while in the opposite direction you may see the outline of the Isle of Wight, 80 miles (128km) away.

For the rest of the way, walking is a delight on springy turf away from all the crowds. There is an energetic switchback at the conclusion, with the cliffs at their most spectacular, before the path comes close to the road at the starting point.

Icklesham from Winchelsea

Start	Winchelsea	
Distance	$6\frac{3}{4}$ miles (10.8km)	
Height gain	510 feet (155m)	
Approximate time	$3\frac{1}{2}$ hours	
Parking	On-street parking near the church in Winchelsea	
Route terrain	Field, woodland and canalside paths; stretches of quiet road	
Ordnance Survey maps	Landranger 189 (Ashford & Romney Marsh), Explorer 124 (Hastings & Bexhill)	

GPS waypoints

Start	TQ 905 173
A	TQ 909 174
B	TQ 895 156
C	TQ 891 156
D	TQ 886 159
E	TQ 876 155
F	TQ 879 164
G	TQ 885 160
H	TQ 894 162

Winchelsea, like its neighbour Rye, is a town crammed full of history, much of it violent. Its streets follow the grid pattern established by Edward I after the destruction of the old town by a storm in 1287. At the start the walk follows the Royal Military Canal, constructed against the threat of Napoleonic invasion, and after this the going is on field paths and a quiet country lane.

Visitors to Winchelsea come to admire its gracious 18th- and 19th-century houses, tidily arranged around the grid of streets laid out by Edward I after a storm had swept away the old town situated on the shoreline. Quays were built on the River Brede, and Winchelsea grew on its hilltop to become a prosperous walled town with 6,000 inhabitants. It was affiliated to the Cinque Ports but its prosperity eventually proved its downfall, attracting French privateers who raided the town repeatedly and massacred the population. In addition, the river began to silt up so that by the 16th-century Winchelsea had lost its access to the sea, leaving the town stranded on its remote hill.

(Start) The walk starts from the church at the centre of the little town, which was designed as the hub of the 13th-century reconstruction. As can be seen, it was originally a much larger building, only the chancel surviving the destruction caused by the French pirates. From the church walk eastwards down the high street to pass the former post office and continue to come to Strand Gate, one of the three surviving gates into the town (the medieval walls have disappeared). From the gate descend Strand Hill and carefully cross the main road at the bottom. Turn right, walk down to the left bend and recross the A259 to the road to Winchelsea Beach.

Cross the Royal Military Canal and take the path on the right (A), to follow the canal's east bank. The canal was excavated in 1804 when the threat of Napoleonic invasion was at its height. It sweeps eastwards in a great arc to Hythe, separating Romney Marsh from inland Kent. It served as a defensive moat and could be used to ferry troops quickly to vulnerable points. There are good views of the town from the banks

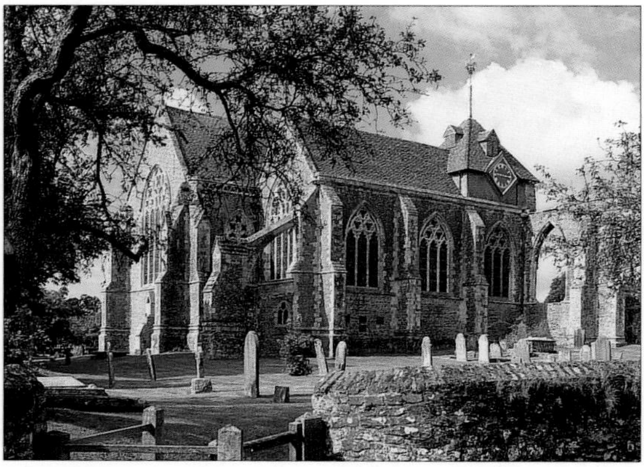

Winchelsea church

of the canal and glimpses of the ruins of Greyfriars monastery through the trees.

The going becomes easier after a stile leads to grazing land. Pass a bridge that takes a footpath over the canal and keep to the bank as it begins to swing left. Cross the wooden footbridge at the end of the bend **B**, avoid the concrete bridge on the right and continue alongside the dyke. Enter the Pannel Valley Nature Reserve and pass a bird hide on the left. Take the next bridge on the right, swing immediately right and then follow the track as it curves to the left between reedbeds to reach a gate near an old concrete outbuilding **C**.

Keep ahead uphill towards a house to a gate at the top and swing left through trees. Turn right on reaching a gate, follow the path over two stiles and cross a drive to a kissing-gate. Go ahead across the field, making for a stile in the right-hand corner, followed by another stile. Keep right in the next field and follow the path to a stile leading out to the lane **D**.

Turn left, following the sign to Pett. There is a view to the left over marshes to Dungeness. There are more lovely views as the quiet lane drops down towards Pannel Bridge. Where the lane levels and turns left, take the track on the right to Little Pannel Farm. The right of way passes the front of the garden and then crosses the field to a metal gate at the top corner **E**. Go through it and over the stile and plank bridge on the left. Bear right up the field, heading to the left of a large cattle shed and pass through the farmyard to a farm drive. Turn left at the end on to a lane that soon reaches the A259 at Icklesham.

Turn right and walk through the village. **The Queen's Head** lies a short distance along Parsonage Lane, a left turning. Opposite the junction is Workhouse Lane. Take this turning and just past the village hall, turn left **F** to follow the 1066 Country Walk waymark. The path passes behind Icklesham church and skirts an orchard before passing to the right of an oast house.

Turn right at the junction then turn left off the tarmac drive to go through the orchard. The postmill soon comes into view. Turn left at a lane after leaving the orchard. After 50 yards go left over a stile G to cross the meadow behind Icklesham windmill. There is a wonderful view from here. Turn left at a lane, but after 125 yards keep ahead to climb a stile and cross a field to the edge of trees. The 1066 Country Walk directs you straight across the field. Cross several stiles and cut off the field corner before reaching a lane H. Cross it and the stile on the other side. The path runs parallel to the lane to another stile and then crosses the field towards Wickham Manor, a lovely 16th-century house. Make for an electricity post to the right of outbuildings and cross stiles and the drive. Now head to the left of New Gate, the southern entry into medieval Winchelsea, to reach the corner of the field, where a stile takes the path over the Town Ditch. Follow the path as it drifts over to the right-hand side of the pasture and begin to approach the field slope. Cross two stiles with a bridleway in between and go left uphill towards a ruined building, the wall of St John's Hospital, an almshouse once belonging to the Friary. Turn right to follow the road to the south side of the churchyard, then first left back to the start. ●

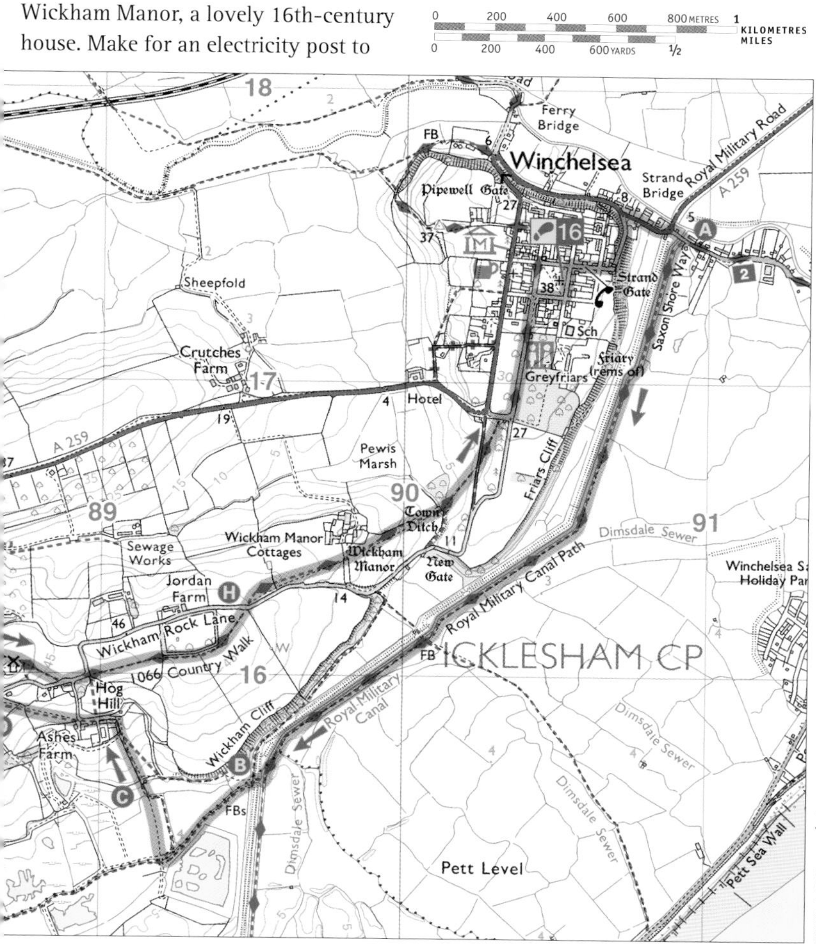

SCALE 1:25000 or 2½ INCHES to 1 MILE *4CM to 1KM*

Groombridge – Through the Medway Valley

Start	Groombridge
Distance	7 miles (11.2km)
Height gain	720 feet (220m)
Approximate time	3½ hours
Parking	At the village hall
Route terrain	Field and woodland paths, former railway
Ordnance Survey maps	Landranger 188 (Maidstone & Royal Tunbridge Wells), Explorer 135 (Ashdown Forest)

GPS waypoints

- TQ 531 373 (start)
- A TQ 524 379
- B TQ 513 379
- C TQ 507 389
- D TQ 500 385
- E TQ 500 375
- F TQ 499 364
- G TQ 523 366

This delightful walk makes a foray into Kent, exploring the Wealdway and well-waymarked border paths through the rolling pastures and woodland either side of the Medway Valley, a lush landscape dotted with oast houses and prosperous farms. An easy final two miles (3.2km) follows the Forest Way along the route of a former railway.

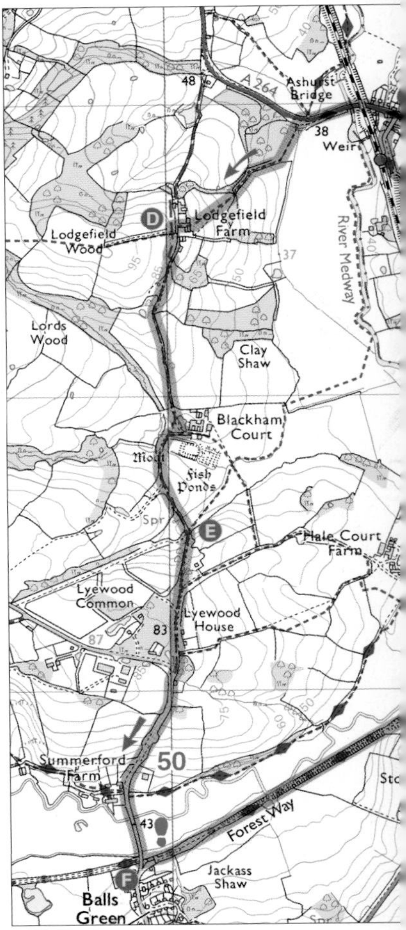

Groombridge straddles the county border with Kent and the old, exceptionally pretty part of the village, in Kent which features 18th-century brick and tile-hung cottages together with a 16th-century inn grouped around a triangular green. Groombridge Place is a fine Jacobean moated mansion set in beautiful 17th-century walled gardens, parkland and forest, which have inspired generations of writers and artists. The formal gardens, patrolled by peacocks, include the drunken topiary garden, the oriental garden and the rose garden.

Pick up the footpath signed to Groombridge Place in the corner of the car park and walk along the left-hand edge of the playing field to a gate. Bear left with the enclosed path, heading gently downhill and soon to bear right towards Groombridge Place.

Cross a bridge and turn immediately left beside the moat to cross the drive and grounds to reach a footbridge. Bear right to pass between a pond and a lake and go through a gate. Bear diagonally left across the field to a gate and cross the B2110 to follow the footway past **The Crown** and along the top of the green. Turn right at the road and head uphill out of the village. Pass the entrance to Quarry House and in 200 yards climb the arrowed stile on your left Ⓐ.

Follow the right-hand field edge for a few paces then bear off left across the centre of the field and cross the drive to Burrswood. Walk through the top edge of woodland and then down through the trees to a stile. Continue straight across the field and drop down into woodland. Cross a track, descend through the wood to a field and follow the path ahead to a further stile. Walk

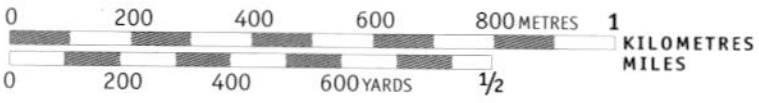

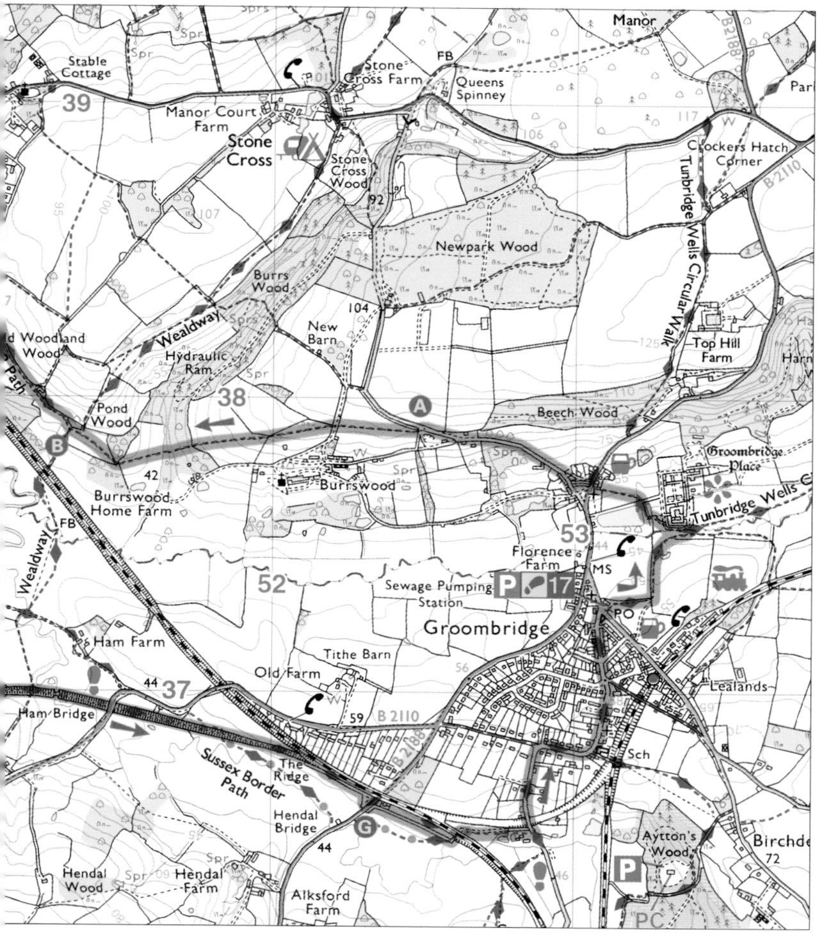

SCALE 1:25 000 or 2½ INCHES to 1 MILE *4CM to 1KM*

through the centre of the next field to reach a Sussex Border Path/Wealdway marker post B.

Continue ahead, gently climbing past a brick building to follow the grassy field-edge path to a stile by a gate. Climb through an avenue of trees, turning left at the top to pass a cottage on the right. Remain on this glorious path to a waymarker post and turn left down a bracken-edged path towards a house. Turn right at the track and follow it as it bears left downhill to emerge in the car park at Ashurst Station. Follow the access road to the A264 C.

Cross the road, turn left along the pavement and cross the River Medway. Re-cross the road and follow the verge for 100 yards to locate a footpath and stile in the lay-by ahead. At the junction of paths take the arrowed path diagonally right through a young plantation. Cross a plank bridge and turn right uphill beside a fence to a stile. Continue uphill across a field towards Lodgefield Farm and locate a stile beside a barn. Cross the farm track ahead, climb some steps and follow the concrete path left to a gate D.

The grassy path soon bears left downhill to join a track on the far side of the farm. Where this curves left into trees, follow the path ahead to a gate. Keep to the left-hand field edge, bearing right at the end of the field to join the tarmac drive to Blackham Court. Follow it away from the house, then where it veers sharp right, take the concrete track ahead uphill through trees to another tarmac drive E.

Turn right then left when you reach the road, walking downhill to pass Summerford Farm and soon cross the River Medway. Just past the 30mph sign on the edge of Balls Green, turn left along the Forest Way F, passing beside the former Withyham Station. The railway line was opened in 1866 and although becoming a busy commuter line, it eventually fell under the axe of the Beeching cuts in 1966. Ironically, Dr Beeching lived near Forest Row and regularly travelled up to London on the line when he was Chairman of British Rail. Now a country park, the 10-mile (16km) long Forest Way is used for walking, cycling and horse riding between East Grinstead and Groombridge.

Follow the route of the old railway, at times close to the meandering River Medway, for a mile (1.6km) to the B2110. Cross the road and continue for a further 1/2 mile (800m) and cross the B2188 on the edge of Groombridge G. The gravel path soon bears left under the railway to reach a lane. Turn left uphill, following it right then left and downhill into the village centre to a T-junction. Cross the road into the car park.

Groombridge Place

Blackboys and Waldron

Start	Blackboys
Distance	7½ miles (12km)
Height gain	640 feet (195m)
Approximate time	3½ hours
Parking	At the village hall
Route terrain	Field and woodland paths; stretches of quiet road
Ordnance Survey maps	Landranger 199 (Eastbourne & Hastings), Explorer OL25 (Eastbourne & Beachy Head)

GPS waypoints

- TQ 521 208
- A TQ 516 203
- B TQ 518 191
- C TQ 537 184
- D TQ 549 192
- E TQ 536 196
- F TQ 524 200

From Blackboys village this generally undemanding ramble follows the waymarked Wealdway long-distance footpath across gently undulating farmland to the quiet hamlet of Waldron, where the Star Inn provides welcome rest and refreshment. The return walk passes through Kiln Wood, a precious remnant of ancient woodland in the care of the Woodland Trust.

Blackboys is located in quiet rural countryside between the Ashdown Forest and the South Downs and its unusual name is thought to be associated with the charcoal-burning industry. It may have derived from the colour of the charcoal burners when they emerged from the woods, but the more likely explanation is that the name means Black Wood, from the soot deposited in the woods by the charcoal. Most of the charcoal probably went to the Buxted Foundry, where the first iron cannon in England was made in 1543. Charcoal burning declined in the 1800s when the iron industry moved north to the Midlands with its large deposits of coal.

Go through the gate at the top of the car park and walk through the allotments, bearing right at the junction of paths to reach a track. Turn left then right in a few paces to follow a fenced path through fields. Beyond a line of holly trees, head downhill towards woodland to a track and turn right. In 50 yards, follow the Wealdway left through a squeeze-stile and along the line of telegraph poles through a clearing to a stile. Follow the fenced path beside a vineyard and continue along a track to reach the B2102. Cross over, turn right along the pavement and then left, following the Wealdway marker along the right-hand field edge to a stile beside a cottage. Turn left along the road and go through the gate on the right in 100 yards A.

Walk down the left-hand field edge to a stile in the corner and bear right along a grass-centred track towards Newplace Farm. Join the concrete track between the house and farm buildings, follow it left and walk down the drive to the road. Turn left then go through the gate on the left, following the left-hand edge of the field ahead. Where the hedge ends strike out across the open field, passing close to a belt of trees on your

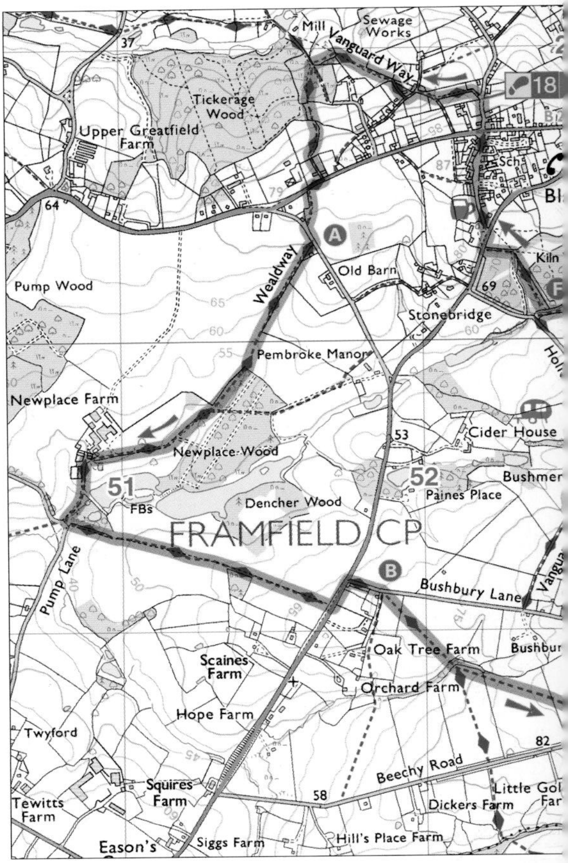

right. Maintain direction to a gate and a road. Turn left, then right along Bushbury Lane, signed to Waldron. Cross a stile on the right to the left of Oak Tree Lodge **B** and head diagonally across the field to a stile and follow the same line to a further stile.

Drop down through a copse, cross a plank bridge and a stile and turn left, leaving the Wealdway, to climb a stile in the hedge. Follow the same line across a succession of fields and stiles, passing in front of a house to cross a stile in the field corner. Turn left along the road to a T-junction, enter the field opposite and bear half right across the field corner to a gate beside woodland. Walk down the field edge to a road and turn left. In 100 yards take the waymarked track right into a field. Turn left, keep left in the next field and then turn right along the field edge in the third field, soon to bear off left towards a way-marker to cross a plank bridge and stile. Continue up the field ahead to a road **C**.

Turn left then right opposite Moat Farm to follow a wide grassy track that eventually reaches a junction of tracks. Cross the track and bear diagonally left along a worn path into the adjoining field. Keep left alongside oak trees and follow the path left into woodland. Exit the trees and continue ahead through the field to a gate and walk across two fields to Waldron church, which

Fields near Newplace Farm

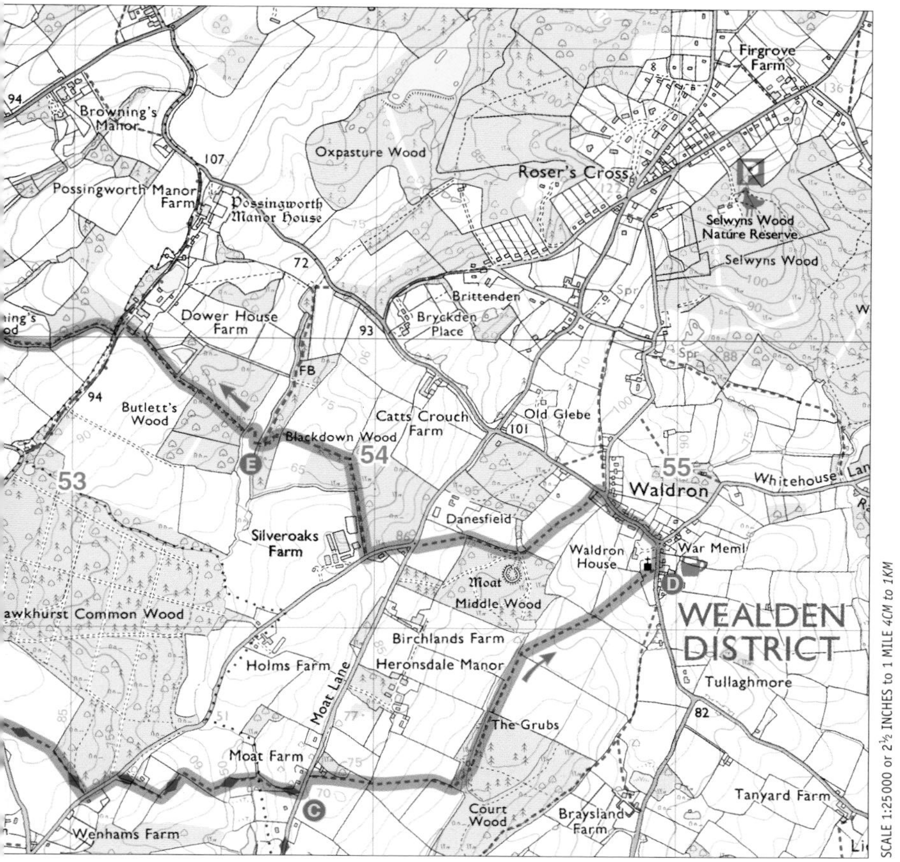

dates from 1195 and contains a fine round Saxon font. Go through the churchyard to the road **D**.

Turn left, pass the **Star Inn** and walk through the village to take the footpath left through the Memorial Hall car park. Walk straight across the playing field, go through a gap in the woodland and follow the path right along the woodland fringe to a stile. Head diagonally across the field to a further stile and road. Walk down Hawkhurst Lane opposite for 200 yards and pass through arrowed gates on your right to join a track (can be muddy) along the edge of woodland. Go through a gate on the left and follow the left-hand field edge to another gate. Keep left at a fork, then right at the next fork, heading

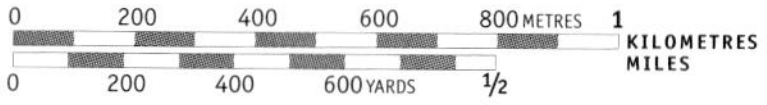

downhill through trees to a gate **E**.

Turn right then left through another gate and head uphill through woodland and along a field edge to pass Dower House Farm. Turn left at a gate, then right in a few paces to follow an enclosed path beside woodland to a gate. Continue and soon enter Browning's Wood and later Kiln Wood, then just before reaching a gate and road, turn right up steps **F** and follow the path to the B2192, opposite the **Blackboys Inn**. Cross over, pass the pub and turn left through the village, keeping ahead at the crossroads back to the village hall.

Friston Forest, the Seven Sisters & Cuckmere Haven

Start	Exceat, Seven Sisters Country Park
Distance	6½ miles (10.5km)
Height gain	1,150 feet (350m)
Approximate time	3½ hours
Parking	Riverside Pay and Display car park at Exceat on south side of A259
Route terrain	Forest tracks, downland, cliff and riverside paths
Ordnance Survey maps	Landranger 199 (Eastbourne & Hastings), Explorer OL25 (Eastbourne & Beachy Head)

GPS waypoints

Start	TV 518 994
A	TV 523 996
B	TV 547 989
C	TV 551 982
D	TV 550 976
E	TV 537 968

Forest, downs, coast and river combine to create a most satisfying and superbly varied walk. A pleasant ramble along wide, green tracks through the woodlands of Friston Forest is followed by a walk across smooth and open downland to reach the coast. Then comes the scenic highlight and most strenuous part of the route: a series of quite steep climbs over four of the Seven Sisters, the succession of chalk cliffs (there are actually eight) that lie just to the west of Beachy Head and one of the most spectacular stretches of coastline in England. After Cuckmere Haven, a gentle stroll by the meandering River Cuckmere makes a relaxing finale.

The spectacular Seven Sisters – where the South Downs meet the sea

The River Cuckmere meandering through the Seven Sisters Country Park

Nowadays Exceat is little more than a name on a map and a few farm buildings by a bridge over the River Cuckmere; the village was abandoned after the Black Death and a series of French raids. Its remains and the site of the church lie buried under fields.

An 18th-century converted barn serves as a visitor centre for the Seven Sisters Country Park, which covers the area of downland, river, estuary and coast to the south.

Turn right out of the car park alongside the busy main road to the bus stop. Cross with care to the paved path and drive opposite by a South Downs Way sign. Head up to a gate, and bearing slightly right continue up the field to the top. There's a fine view from here looking back over the Cuckmere meanders. Go through another gate and climb a stone stile in the wall, bearing right then left to enter Friston Forest, a delightful area of mixed woodland managed by the Forestry Commission. Descend a long flight of steps into the sleepy and unspoilt village. At the bottom, keep ahead at the path intersection to the lane **A**. Turn right along it following it round to the left. Just before reaching a Friston Forest sign, a short detour to the left brings you to the small, plain church with the short tower and spire typical of Sussex.

Keep ahead along the lane, heading uphill into woodland again, where the tarmac lane becomes a forest track. Now follow this lovely, broad, grassy track for nearly 1½ miles (2.4km) through the forest. At a fork take the right-hand uphill track, in the Friston direction, and later, where the roughly made-up forest track veers left, go ahead on a grassy path. Descend to cross a track, continue uphill again, keeping along the right-hand edge of an area of open grassland, and finally head downhill to pass beside a barrier onto a tarmac drive **B**.

Turn left and just after the drive bends right take the narrow path that runs parallel to it on the left. At a waymark post, following the footpath signed for Friston and East Dean, turn right across the drive up the steps opposite and through a gate. Keep straight ahead across a field, go through a gate on the far side and descend steps to a tarmac drive. Cross it, bear slightly left to climb the stile opposite and continue diagonally and slightly uphill across a field to another stile in the far corner. Climb it and follow a path through woodland, finally climbing a stone stile on the left to reach a road near to its junction with the main road **C**. Go over the road and grass beyond to the main road.

Cross the busy main road with care and take the no-through road opposite signposted for Crowlink, passing between a lily pond on the right and Friston's small, attractive church on the left. If visibility is poor, carry straight on down the access road to Crowlink. Otherwise just before entering the National Trust's Crowlink car park, turn left through a gate and then turn half-right across a field. Go through a gate and bear right along a very indistinct path **D**, keeping in a straight line diagonally across the field. Although the numerous paths across this National Trust property may appear confusing, there is no problem. Once you reach the brow of a hill, aim for the hamlet buildings spotted through the trees below. Look out for a stile in a wire fence, climb it and continue downhill to pass through a hedge gap onto the access lane. Turn left passing to the right of the cottages, go through a gate and walk through the dry valley of Gap Bottom, keeping by a wire fence and hedge on the right. Continue along a wide, smooth, grassy path that winds through the shallow valley bottom to the edge of the cliffs **E**.

Turn right onto the South Downs Way to Cuckmere Haven, a route that climbs over four of the series of chalk cliffs known as the Seven Sisters. There are

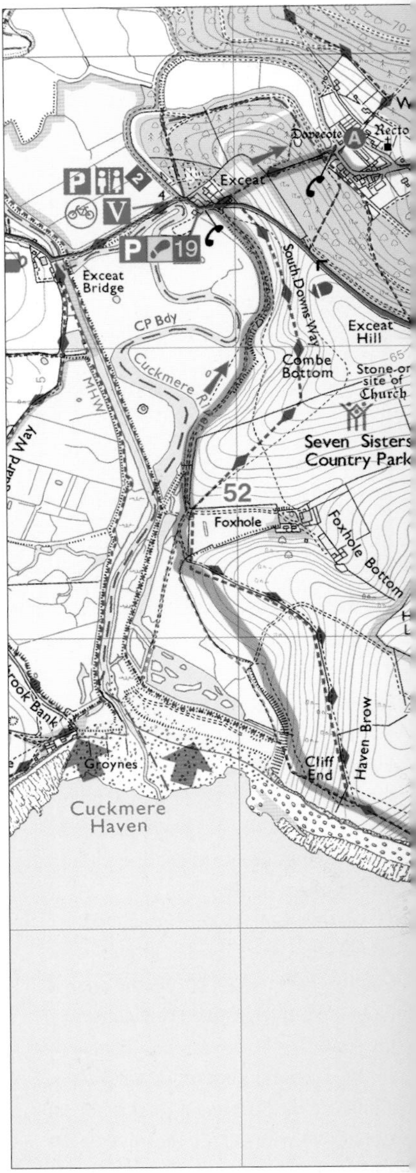

some steep 'ups and downs' on this section but the superb cliff scenery and the magnificent, extensive views more than compensate for the effort expended. Over the last brow you look down on Cuckmere Haven, the beautiful and unspoilt estuary of the Cuckmere, with its shingle beach, lagoons and meandering river, and beyond that to Seaford Head.

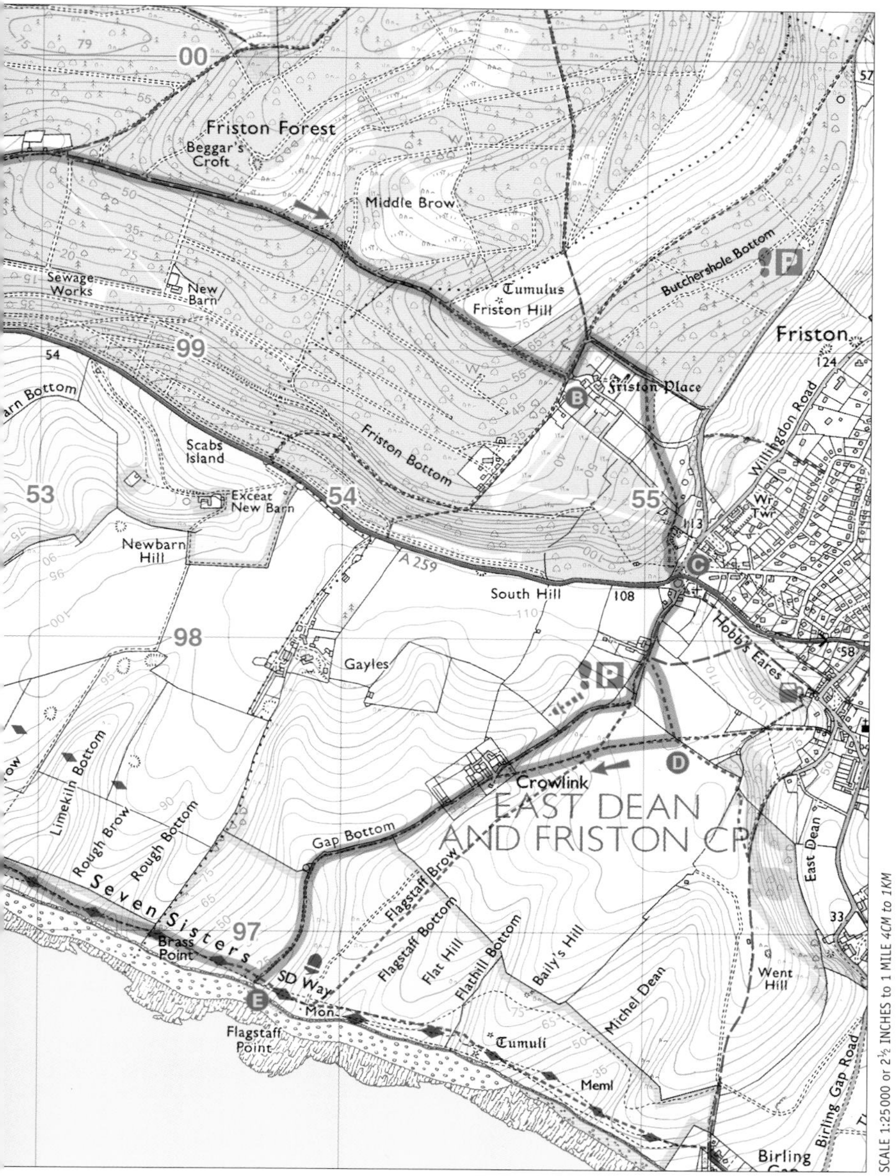

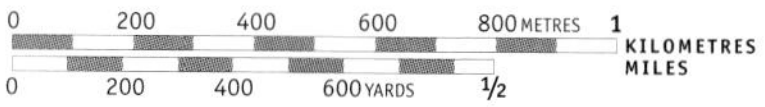

Descend steeply towards the beach and just before the final, steep descent, turn right through a gate and along the side of the valley above the river. Head downhill along a pleasant, grassy path, go through a gate on the left and bear right.

At a T-junction of tracks bear right, go through a gate and continue along a concrete track to the right of the marshes, lagoons and meanders of the Cuckmere, among the finest river meanders in Britain. In 1846 this section of the river was straightened and canalised to reduce flooding. As you near Exceat, bear left onto a grassy track, back to the car park. ●

Mayfield and Wadhurst Park

		GPS waypoints
Start	Mayfield	TQ 587 269
Distance	$8\frac{1}{4}$ miles (13.2km)	A TQ 595 280
Height gain	870 feet (265m)	B TQ 601 290
Approximate time	4 hours	C TQ 611 293
Parking	Car park in the village centre	D TQ 619 286
Route terrain	Field and woodland paths	E TQ 630 278
Dog friendly	Keep dogs on lead through Wadhurst Deer Park	F TQ 628 266
		G TQ 609 271
		H TQ 594 264
Ordnance Survey maps	Landranger 188 (Maidstone & Royal Tunbridge Wells), Explorer 136 (High Weald, Royal Tunbridge Wells)	

From the lofty and attractive village of Mayfield, this peaceful ramble explores the glorious High Weald landscape to the east of the village, following the tranquil Tidebrook Valley to Wadhurst Park, with its huge herd of deer and wildlife-rich lake. The walk returns through an isolated valley that was once the site of the Hawksden Forge Iron Smelter, which gave Mayfield its prosperity during the 16th and 17th centuries.

Mayfield is a thriving High Weald village situated on a breezy ridge with panoramic views south across rolling countryside towards Burwash. It has a fine main street with raised redbrick pavements and some notable old houses, including **The Middle House**, a splendid oak-timbered Tudor inn dating back to 1576. The mainly perpendicular Church of St Dunstan displays a 16th-century screen and a tall spire. Two cast iron tomb slabs in the nave reflect the importance of the iron industry in the valleys around the village.

From the car park entrance walk up the lane opposite to reach the High Street and turn right. Follow the road left and soon take the footpath right across the Memorial Hall car park to join a tarmac path to the right of the hall, with great views across the High Weald. Where the path forks, curving left to a skateboard park, keep ahead down the grass to the wooded corner of the football pitch, descend steps and cross a track and stile. Continue through the field to a stile by a gate and keep ahead at a crossing of paths down the right-hand edge of a field to a stile. Descend beside woodland and follow the path down into Vicarage Wood, bearing slightly right down to a waymarker post. Bear left to cross a footbridge, then bear immediately right into rough scrubland and keep left uphill beside the wood to reach a large field A.

Bear left and follow the path across

the gently rising field and the field beyond, then follow the right-hand edge of the next field beside woodland. Where a narrower grassy path forks right, follow this to a stile/path leading into woodland. Swing right then left down to a footbridge. Cross the bridge and turn immediately left at the fork of paths. Exit the trees into a field via a footbridge and keep right beside woodland to a kissing-gate. Continue straight on, passing a group of silver birch trees, to climb through the centre of a field to a stile and road B. Go through the gateway opposite, pass between cottages and keep ahead at a fork by a gate to cross the stile ahead. Follow the left-hand field edge and soon drop down left through a field towards woodland to a waymarked gate at the bottom. Go through the next gate by a corrugated barn and walk towards the house ahead. Pass in front of Mousehall and follow the drive, keeping right at the junction to pass Mousehall Mill and follow the track to the road. Turn right, then left in 200 yards along a track C, signed to Chittinghurst.

Remain on this track past buildings at Chittinghurst, the track eventually reaching a footbridge and a gate. Keep ahead to the far right-hand corner of the field, go through two gates D at a crossing of paths and continue ahead along the field edge to a footbridge, then drop down to a plank bridge, with Combe Farm away to your left. Follow the yellow arrows, soon to walk beside a stream to reach a drive and turn left across the concrete bridge. Follow the waymarker right beside a pond, cross a stile and proceed straight across the field ahead on a path continuing through the next field to reach a gate by an oak tree. Enter Wadhurst Deer Park, walk ahead uphill to reach a gravel track and follow it right with Wadhurst Park Lake away to your left. Cross a bridge and bear left, following the waymarkers through the parkland to eventually reach a gate by Batt's Wood E.

Go through the gate and turn immediately right alongside the wood, keeping ahead at an information board. On nearing a house, follow the diverted path left through the trees and skirt a deep dell to reach a wide grassy path. Follow the path right, cross a stile and follow the field edge downhill, soon joining the gravel drive. Remain on the undulating track down to where it veers sharp left in the bottom of a valley F. The stream in this valley feeds the upper Rother Valley and played an important part in developing the prosperity of Mayfield. Two key iron smelting forges (Hawksden and Bivelham) were located in the valleys, the stream powering the bellows

Looking across Wadhurst Deer Park

that heated the locally produced charcoal to melt the iron.

Turn right along a wooded path, go through a kissing-gate and follow the path along the raised bank ahead, soon to pass between an oast house and a farmhouse (Hare Holt). Join the tarmac drive and soon bear off right at a fork to join a bridleway. Ignore steps on your right, and bear right at a fork just before a stone bridge to cross a stile by a gate. Walk through a narrow field, bearing right to a stile and follow the path ahead uphill through trees to a gate. Turn left, cross a stile in front of a white weatherboarded cottage (Hampden Lodge), and follow the track ahead through the peaceful valley. At a pond and waymarker post turn left into a field and keep right over a ditch and keep right through the valley bottom field. Go through a gate, cross a drive and pass to the left of garages to reach a stile. Continue ahead parallel with the

stream to cross a stile and footbridge, then keep right where a path merges from the left **G**.

The bridleway steadily climbs for ½ mile (800m) to join a wide gravel track, bearing right to reach the road. Turn left for 200 yards and turn right along Piccadilly Lane, a quiet single-track road. Pass Piccadilly Farm and take the footpath right over a stile at a driveway **H**. Take the right-hand path downhill beside the fenced orchard on the left. Drop down through the trees to cross a footbridge and continue up the left-hand edge of the field beyond. Maintain direction along the edge of the next field and through the following, then along an enclosed field to houses near a road junction. Turn left along the lane (The Avenue), keeping ahead/right at a fork back to the car park. ●

0 200 400 600 800 METRES 1 KILOMETRES
0 200 400 600 YARDS ½ MILES

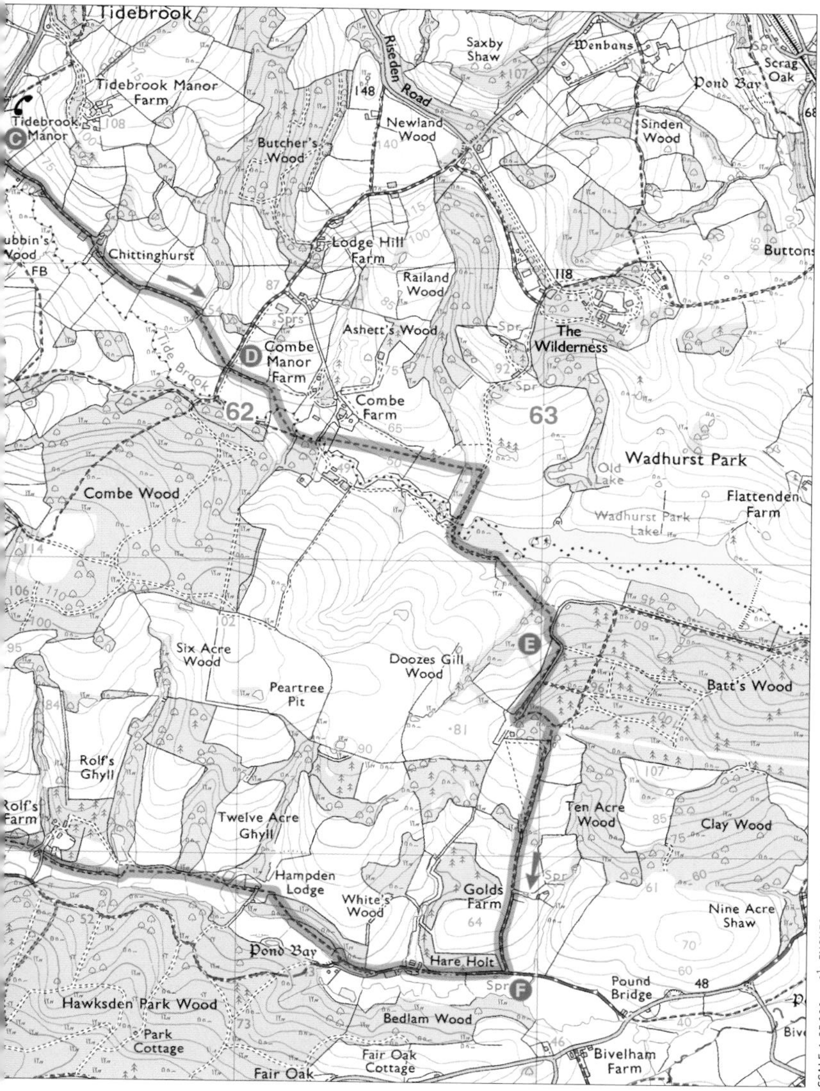

SCALE 1:25000 or 2½ INCHES to 1 MILE *4CM to 1KM*

Alfriston, Long Man of Wilmington and Jevington

Start	Alfriston
Distance	8¼ miles (13.2km)
Height gain	1,195 feet (365m)
Approximate time	4 hours
Parking	The Willow long-stay Pay and Display car park on the left of the main road on the northern approach to town
Route terrain	Downland tracks; short section of riverside path
Ordnance Survey maps	Landranger 199 (Eastbourne & Hastings), Explorer OL25 (Eastbourne & Beachy Head)

GPS waypoints

Start	TQ 520 031
A	TQ 522 031
B	TQ 532 032
C	TQ 544 042
D	TQ 558 038
E	TQ 563 019
F	TQ 561 014
G	TQ 532 019
H	TQ 525 026

An ancient, mysterious chalk figure and four highly attractive and distinctive villages, all with fine medieval churches, are linked by this energetic walk on the South Downs that starts and finishes in the beautiful Cuckmere Valley. It combines the best of downland scenery with considerable historic appeal and offers many grand and extensive views across open, rolling country. There is plenty of climbing but nothing steep or strenuous.

A number of factors combine to make Alfriston one of the most appealing villages in Sussex. It is attractively situated below the downs on the west bank of the lovely River Cuckmere, and from the old market cross its narrow main street slopes gently downhill, lined with old houses, shops, tearooms and medieval inns. Across a charming open grassy area called the Tye stands the unusually imposing and sturdy-looking cruciform church, the 'Cathedral of the Downs', overlooking riverside meadows. Beside the church is the thatched, timber-framed, 14th-century Clergy House, which was the first building acquired by the National Trust, in 1896. Until the 18th century Alfriston was a port, and its comparative

isolation near a lonely stretch of coast made it an ideal smuggling centre.

The walk begins at the market cross in the village centre. Walk down the main street, turn left along a tarmac path beside the United Reformed Church – there are footpath signs to the Tye and War Memorial Hall – and after passing the church bear slightly left to continue between walls. To the right across the Tye are the medieval church and Clergy House. Keep ahead to cross a footbridge over the River Cuckmere, turn left Ⓐ, pass through a gate and continue along a raised embankment above low-lying meadowland, parallel to the river.

Go through a gate to the right of a brick bridge, turn right along a lane to a T-junction and continue ahead along a track, following a South Downs Way sign. After passing the entrance to a house the track narrows to a sunken hedge–and tree-lined path that heads uphill and bears left to a lane Ⓑ. Cross over, continue along the track ahead, go through a gate and follow the track uphill onto open downland. Soon there are fine views to the coast. Pass right of a reservoir and aerial. Go through another gate and continue, bearing right to a junction of tracks.

Here turn sharp left, almost doubling back, and head downhill with a wire fence and tumulus on the right. After 100 yards turn right through a gate and walk along a path, by a wire fence on the left, that heads across the slopes of Windover Hill to pass below the Long Man of Wilmington. In front of the chalk figure bear left to a gate. The Long Man, 230 feet (70m) long and cut from the chalk downland, is claimed to be the largest representation of the human figure in western Europe. His origins are obscure: he could be prehistoric, Saxon or medieval and many theories

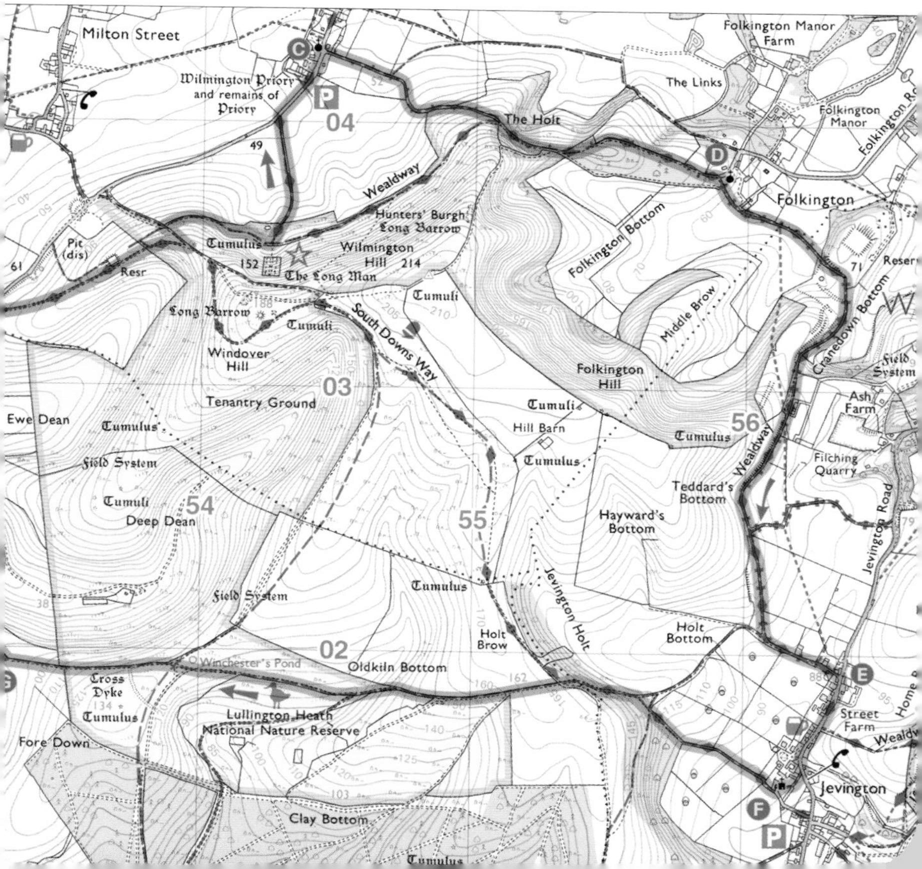

abound. The first drawings of him come from an 18th-century manuscript where the two staffs that he is holding are shown as a rake and scythe, which suggests that he was perhaps an agricultural fertility figure.

Go through the gate and follow the path ahead gently downhill, going through another gate onto a lane. Turn right to Wilmington Priory – there is a parallel footpath on the right which rejoins the lane opposite the priory and Long Man car park. The small 12th-century church next to the priory was a dual purpose building, serving the needs of both the local people and the monks of the priory; there were so few monks that a separate church was considered unnecessary. Although the church is predominantly Norman, the nave was rebuilt in the 14th century, and the whole building was extensively restored by the Victorians. At the west end is the usual belfry and short spire commonly found in Sussex. Note the giant ancient yew in the churchyard. Wilmington Priory is now a museum.

Opposite the church turn right **C**, at a public bridleway sign to Folkington, along a partially tree-and hedge-lined track that winds uphill, eventually entering woodland. Bear left and continue through the attractive woodland. Later the track narrows to a path and keeps along the edge of the trees, giving excellent views to the left across the Weald, eventually heading gently downhill to a T-junction **D**. In front is Folkington's tiny, simple church.

At the T-junction, bear right along a downhill, tree-lined track and continue along an enclosed path that heads steadily uphill, curving gradually to the right and later straightens out and continues gently downhill. After 1¼ miles (2km) at a T-junction, turn left along the track into Jevington. Turn right **E** along the road through the village and, where it bears slightly left to head downhill, continue along a path that leads into the churchyard. The church is a delightful building in a lovely spot overlooking the downs. Its west tower is Saxon, and during restoration work in 1875 a Saxon sculpture was discovered in the building.

Walk past the church and turn right **F** at a bridleway sign to Alfriston and a South Downs Way acorn symbol, along a hedge-lined path that heads gently uphill and continues along the right, inside edge of woodland. Keep ahead at a South Downs Way sign and about 50 yards farther on bear left on joining a track. Continue steadily uphill through woodland and on emerging from the trees you reach a bridle-way post. Here the South Downs Way turns right but you keep straight ahead.

Now there is a splendid stretch of walking along a fairly straight, undulating track across open, breezy downland, with extensive views over the downs and the thick, dark woodlands of Friston Forest to the left, passing Lullington Heath National Nature Reserve, an area of conserved chalk down. Keep straight on at a waymark in the Litlington direction, at the next bridleway sign keep ahead, but where the track forks at the next sign take the right-hand track **G** towards Lullington Court.

As you head downhill there is a fine view of Alfriston in front. The track becomes hedge-lined and eventually curves slightly right to reach a road. Turn right, take the first turning on the left **H**, signposted to Alfriston, and where the road bears slightly right keep ahead through a gate.

Walk along the right-hand edge of a meadow, by a hedge on the right; from here there is a lovely view across the meadow and river to Alfriston church and the Clergy House. Climb a stile and continue along a hedge-enclosed path to a crossing of paths. Turn left onto a tarmac path and cross the Cuckmere into Alfriston.

Blackcap and Stanmer Down from Ditchling Beacon

Start	Ditchling Beacon
Distance	8½ miles (13.7km)
Height gain	900 feet (275m)
Approximate time	4 hours
Parking	At start (Pay and Display)
Route terrain	Downland tracks and woodland paths
Ordnance Survey maps	Landranger 198 (Brighton & Lewes), Explorer OL11 (Brighton & Hove)

GPS waypoints

Start	TQ 333 129
A	TQ 370 125
B	TQ 384 118
C	TQ 376 112
D	TQ 363 110
E	TQ 350 098
F	TQ 347 108

At 813 feet (248m) the Ditchling Beacon is the third-highest summit on the South Downs. The beacon gave warning of the coming of the Armada in 1588. The route follows the South Downs Way at first – a National Trail, which, as a long-distance bridleway, is open to cyclists and horses as well as walkers. The Way turns off southwards near Blackcap, and the walking is then through comparatively deserted countryside where some careful map-reading may be needed.

The land around the Beacon was given to the National Trust to serve as a monument to a young pilot shot down in the Second World War.

Cross the road from the car park and head eastwards along the South Downs Way, passing a dew pond on the right. The view to the north is an early highlight of the walk. At first the going is excellent on springy turf over Western Brow, keeping on the crest of the hill to eventually cross a tarmac lane atop Streat Hill. Keeping ahead the surface underfoot becomes flinty on a rough track. The village of Plumpton lies below with its sprawling agricultural college.

After walking for nearly an hour you will enter the National Trust's Blackcap property. Here the South Downs Way leaves to the right A. Keep ahead through the gate onto open downland and about 100 yards past the junction, bear right at a fork (the left fork heads up to the trig point on Blackcap). A lonely post marks a bridleway crossways – keep to the main track going ahead to come to a gate by an electricity pylon. Go through the gate and, after 80 yards, turn sharp right B by a National Trust sign onto a bridleway (muddy in winter) leading through woodland.

After about 250 yards turn right through a gate and follow the waymarked bridleway diagonally across

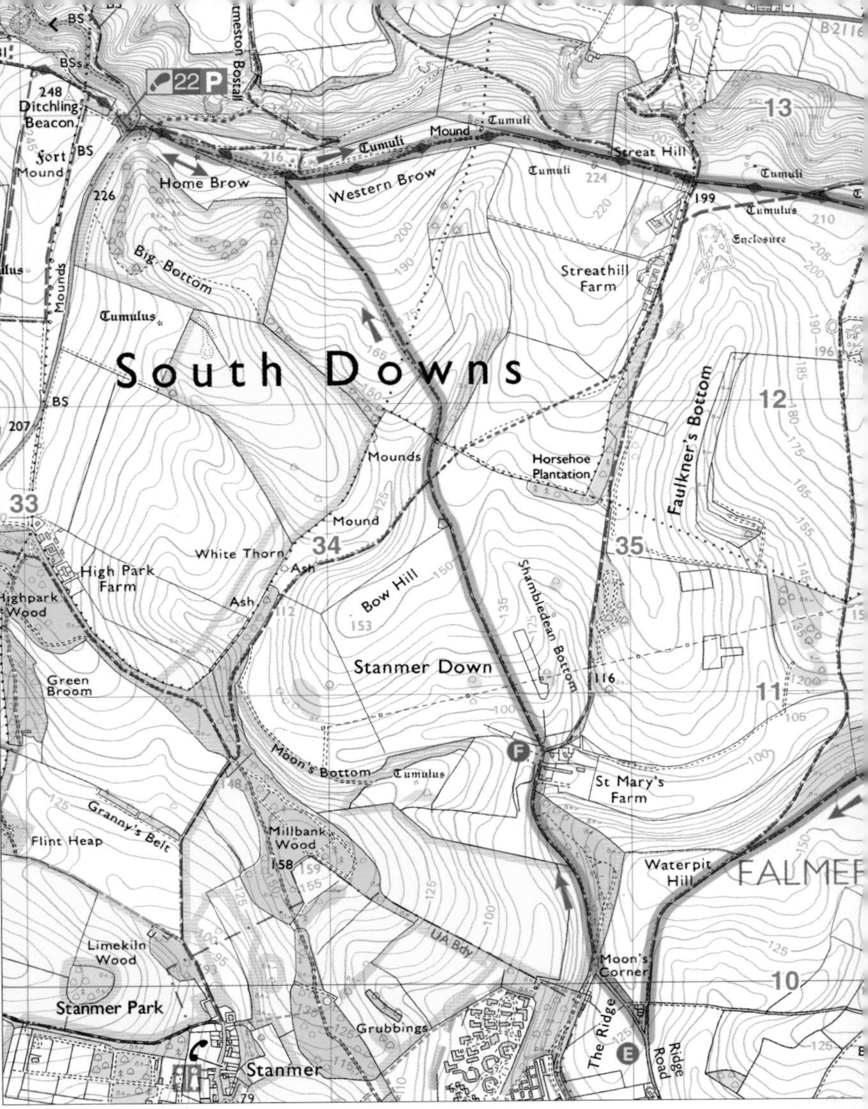

a field to the old gate posts in the former fence ahead. Continue to the far corner of the field and go through another gate. Carry on beside the hedge on the right to a waymark post and gap in the trees. Turn right and descend to a path intersection at the bottom of the valley **C**.

Cross a track to a gate and from here climb to the former gateway near the top of a tree-topped knoll. This will prove to be a false summit as the path continues to climb after the wooded area. Keep ahead along the field edge to reach a junction with a wide track, the South Downs Way. Bear right and a few paces on fork left through a gate. From here, the right of way – a very faint path in the grass – swings in an arc close to a line of scrubby bushes to reach a waymarked wooden gate **D**.

Go through the gate, cross the track and the neck of the field beyond it, then turn left onto a grassy track by the fence that leads past a small wood. After this there is a lovely view to the right over St Mary's Farm; a bridleway joins from the right, and the track bears

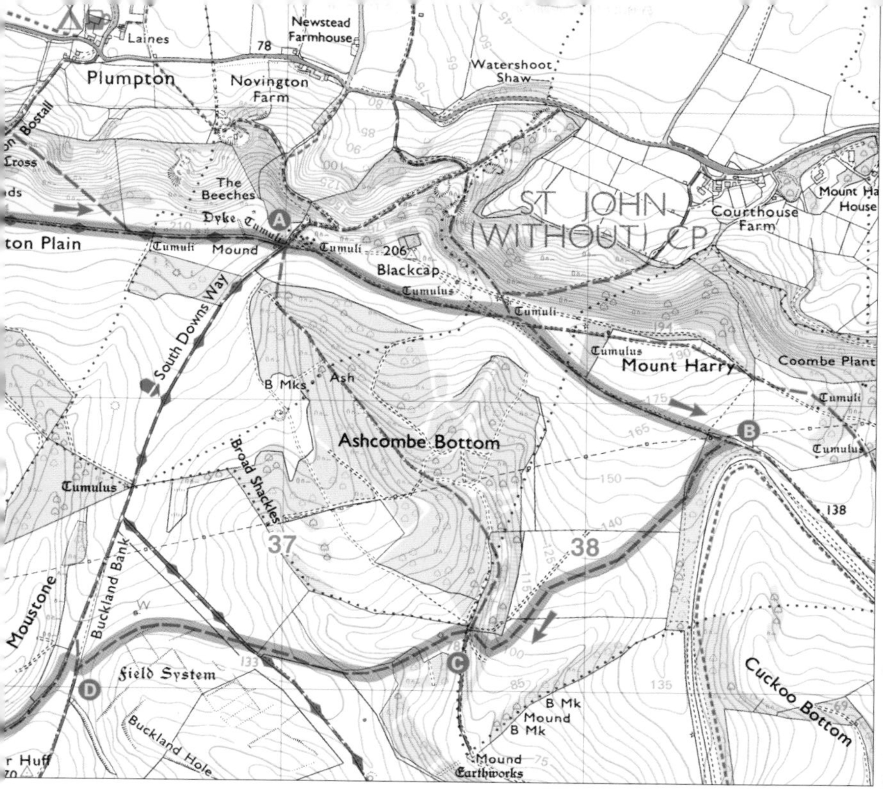

SCALE 1:25000 or 2½ INCHES to 1 MILE *4CM to 1KM*

0 200 400 600 800 METRES 1 KILOMETRES
0 200 400 600 YARDS ½ MILES

left, gently descending Waterpit Hill.

At the junction with Ridge Road about ½ mile (800m) to the north of Falmer (the University of Sussex falls within the parish), turn right **E** up the lane and then follow it downhill. Once clear of the trees on the left, looking back you can see the university buildings. At the bottom continue past St Mary's Farmhouse and the cottages and as the track curves right keep ahead through a gate **F**. The track crests the flank of Stanmer Down and continues through a gate along the left-hand field edge. A gate in the left-hand hedge marks a crossways, before the path drops through a wooden gate into a small sequestered valley.

Follow the path as it curves gently left up to a further gate, continuing steadily up the grassy hillside over the left-hand flank of Western Brow. At the top, go through the gate rejoining the South Downs Way and turn left and retrace your outward steps to the Beacon.

Looking out from Ditchling Beacon

Arlington and Abbot's Wood

Start	Arlington Reservoir
Distance	8½ miles (13.6km)
Height gain	375 feet (115m)
Approximate time	4 hours
Parking	Pay and Display car park
Route terrain	Field and woodland paths
Ordnance Survey maps	Landranger 199 (Eastbourne & Hastings), Explorer OL25 (Eastbourne & Beachy Head)

GPS waypoints

- Start: TQ 528 074
- A: TQ 543 081
- B: TQ 552 099
- C: TQ 561 094
- D: TQ 566 091
- E: TQ 562 084
- F: TQ 557 072
- G: TQ 543 074

An easy, level walk that follows the Wealdway across farmland, close to the Cuckmere River, to Michelham Priory, a beautiful moated historic house, before returning through Abbot's Wood to Arlington village. Allow time to visit the interesting flint Church of St Pancras and enjoy a spot of bird watching from the hide beside Arlington Reservoir.

Completed in 1971 to supply 23 million litres of water daily to the Eastbourne and Hailsham areas, Arlington Reservoir is also an important local nature reserve, a favoured haunt for many migrant birds, including the Osprey, and a wintering ground for up to 10,000 wildfowl.

(Start) Cross the grassy area in front of the car park and bear left to follow the lower path beside the reservoir. Keep ahead where the path merges with a bridleway and soon reach a fork of paths by an information board. Follow the fence ahead to a gate and keep to the left-hand field edge, passing beneath power cables. Follow the field edge right and soon pass in front of Sessingham Farm to cross a driveway and footbridge. Follow the bridleway right to reach a bridge (A) over the Cuckmere River.

Climb the stile just before the bridge to join the Wealdway and walk parallel with the river. Go though a gate,

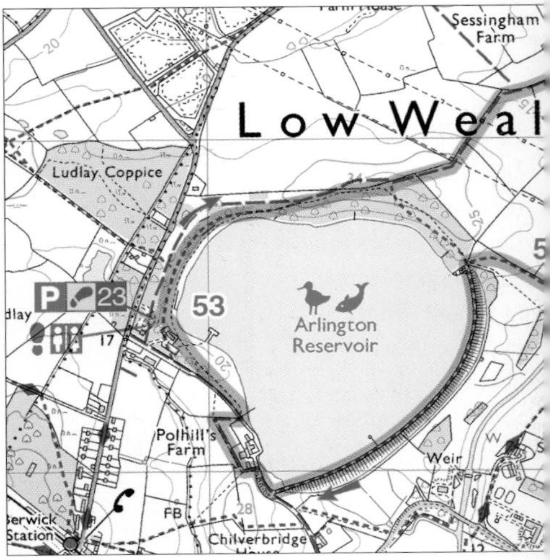

continue along the right-hand field edge, soon to bear half-left across the open field, keeping right of the telegraph pole and oak trees to locate a footbridge on the field edge. Cross the footbridge, bear left to a stile and walk across two fields to reach a stile to the right of a brick cottage. Turn left along the tarmac drive, then almost immediately cross the stile on the right and walk beside the woodland to a stile in the field corner. Keep ahead along the edge of the golf course, cross a stile by a noticeboard and then the stile ahead to follow a hedged path right to reach the road. Turn right into Upper Dicker, passing **The Plough** and St Bede's School before following the Wealdway right just before the village shop Ⓑ.

Pass between houses to a stile, cross a paddock and a further stile and plank bridge, then bear slightly right across a playing field to another stile. Keep left along the field edge, cross a stile and turn left to follow a diagonal path to the far end of farm buildings and a track. Turn left over the bridge at the edge of

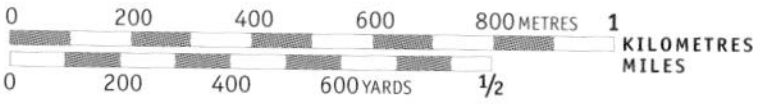

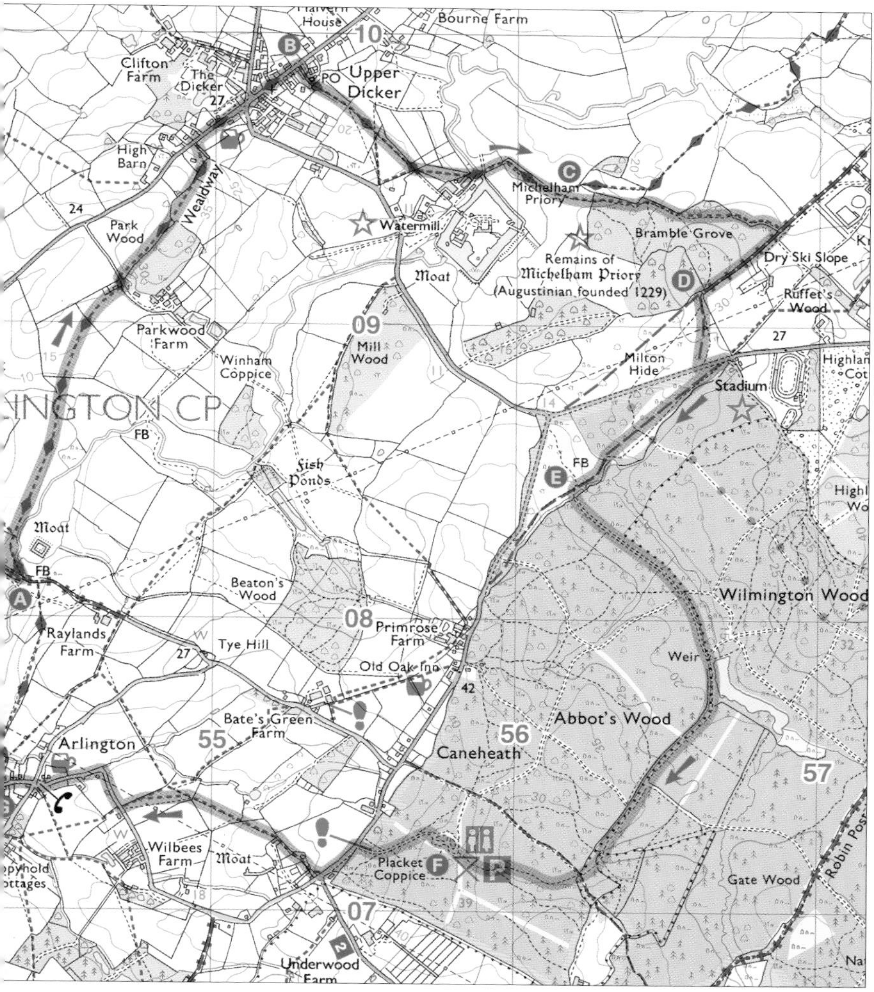

SCALE 1:25000 or 2½ INCHES to 1 MILE *4CM to 1KM*

Towards Arlington church

England's longest water-filled medieval moat, which surrounds Michelham Priory (hidden in trees). The Priory was founded in 1229 for 12 canons and a prior and includes the remains of the former Augustinian priory (open), a Tudor mansion filled with furniture and artefacts, a 14th-century gatehouse, a medieval watermill, and a dramatic Elizabethan Great Barn. Continue to cross a second bridge and follow the Wealdway right through a narrow field to a gate C.

Leave the Wealdway, bearing half-left to a stile on the edge of Bramble Grove. Follow the path through the wood to a gate and turn right around the field edge to a stile. Follow the wide byway right and head uphill beside woodland. At the top of the rise D bear left downhill to reach a road.

Turn left, then in 100 yards take the arrowed path sharp right and follow the line of telegraph poles through a clearing on the edge of Wilmington Wood. As it widens, keep left of the wires to locate a bridleway that descends into the wood to cross a footbridge. Look out for a green barrier E on the left and follow the forest track beyond it into Abbot's Wood, a mixed woodland of approximately 360 hectares that derives its name from the times of Henry I, when the wood was gifted to Battle Abbey and overseen by the Abbot (hence Abbot's Wood).

Keep ahead at a crossing towards 'The Lake' and remain on the main path as it skirts the lake and curves right through the wood. Continue ahead on merging with a track, do the same at the next junction and descend to a crossing of paths. Follow the narrower path ahead to reach the car park F.

Exit the wood via the tarmac access road and turn left to reach a road junction. Take the footpath over a stile on the right beyond the post box. Cross the stiles and drive to your left and turn right along the field edge to a stile. Keep ahead, soon to bear left around the field edge to reach a stile in a hedge on your right. Go straight across the field ahead to double stiles, then fork left to a stile and road. Turn right into Arlington, bearing right at the **Yew Tree Inn** to the church G.

Walk through the churchyard, bear left to a gate and follow the path ahead to cross a stile. Turn right, cross the footbridge over the Cuckmere River and head uphill to the reservoir. Pass through the gate (bird hide signed right) and turn left along the reservoir wall to a track. Turn right, skirt around Polhill's Farm on a fenced path, then cross the track to follow the grassy path close to the reservoir back to the car park.

Sussex Border Paths from Fletching

Start	Fletching
Distance	$9\frac{1}{4}$ miles (15km)
Height gain	705 feet (215m)
Approximate time	$4\frac{1}{2}$ hours
Parking	Car park opposite the Griffin Inn
Route terrain	Field and woodland paths; stretches of quiet road
Ordnance Survey maps	Landranger 198 (Brighton & Lewes), Explorer 135 (Ashdown Forest)

GPS waypoints

- Start: TQ 429 235
- A: TQ 421 249
- B: TQ 415 257
- C: TQ 406 263
- D: TQ 396 258
- E: TQ 390 246
- F: TQ 391 239
- G: TQ 405 236
- H: TQ 410 222

This rewarding ramble explores the gently rolling Wealden countryside between the Ouse Valley and the Ashdown Forest. From wooded valleys and open fields with South Downs views you can also enjoy a rural museum and, if you want to make a day of it, experience a steam train ride along the Bluebell Railway, or visit the National Trust's Sheffield Park Gardens.

Almost as old as neighbouring Ashdown Forest, Fletching is an attractive village with a 13th-century church and the oldest licensed inn (The Griffin) in Sussex, which dates from 1150. Simon de Montfort's army camped outside the church prior to the Battle of Lewes in 1256.

(Start) Leaving the car park, turn right along the village street and head north out of the village. Go through the gate opposite Atherall's Farm and follow the farm track to a gate. Bear half-left to a further gate and keep right along the field edge to a waymarker and gate on the left. Walk straight across the field to a gate and lane, opposite Spring Farm. Turn left, then in 500 yards bear off right along a footpath through a belt of trees (A).

Cross a drive, walk through the copse then bear half-left across a field, dropping down to a junction of tracks. Walk along the edge of the field opposite, parallel with a track, and soon reach a junction of paths in woodland. Turn right, then left at a junction of paths by a lake to pass Sheffield Mill Farm. Join the drive (B) and follow it uphill to a lane. Turn right and eventually descend on the sunken lane to take the signed hedged track left. Cross the A275 and follow the drive to Heaven Farm (C) where 180 years of farming life in the Sussex Weald are preserved through a collection of rural farm machinery and artefacts housed in a beautiful old barn.

Pass between the **tearoom** and the gift shop and bear right in front of a barn, signed Nature Trail. Pass a pond, then walk uphill along the right-hand field edge, passing the Wellingtonia tree marking the Greenwich Meridian. With views of the South Downs continue to the top of the field and turn right through trees to a stile. Turn left and immediately fork left into the next field,

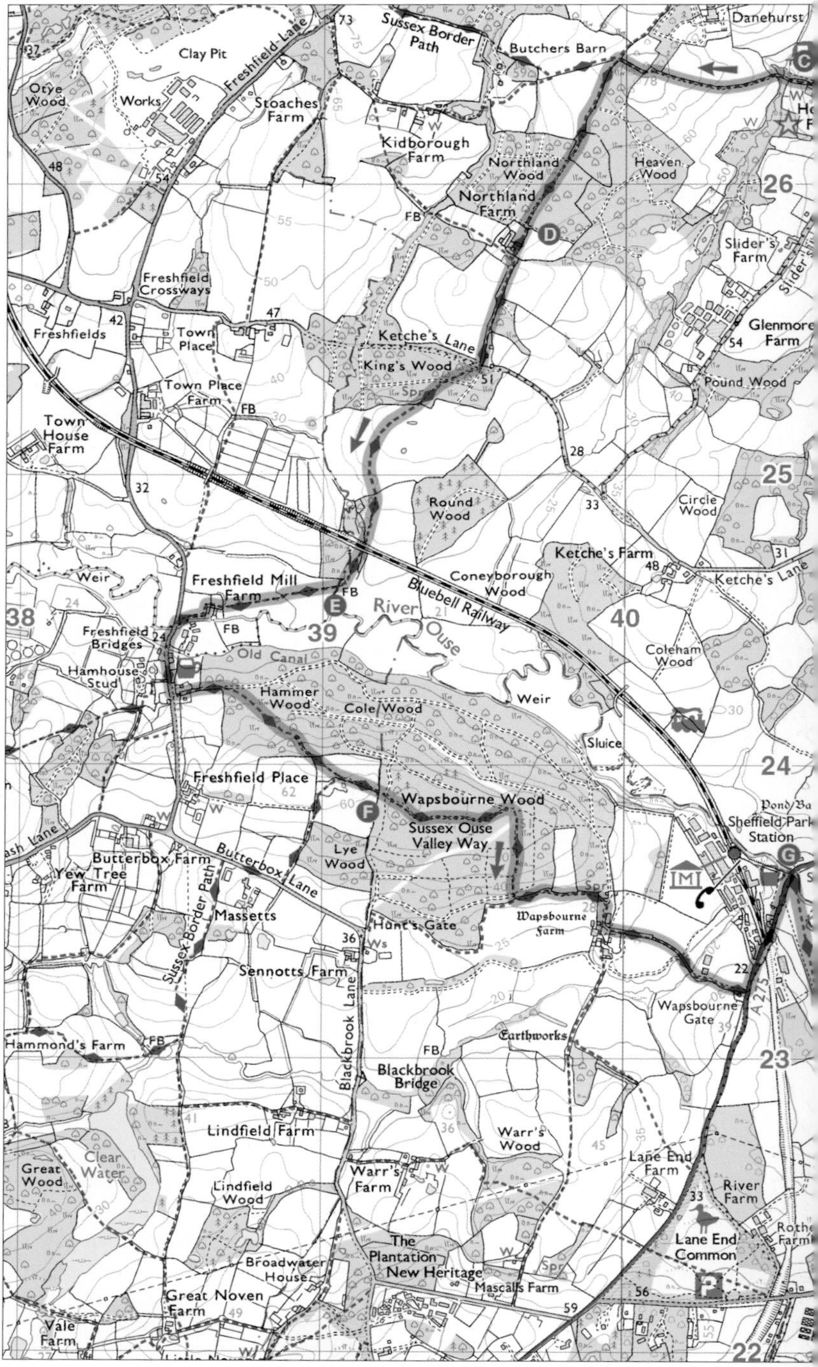

following the Sussex Border Path beside woodland to a stile. Walk through Northland Wood. Exit the trees (D), pass

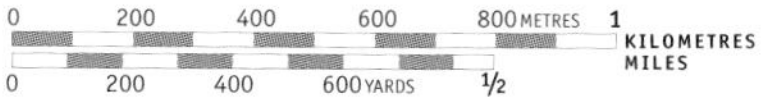

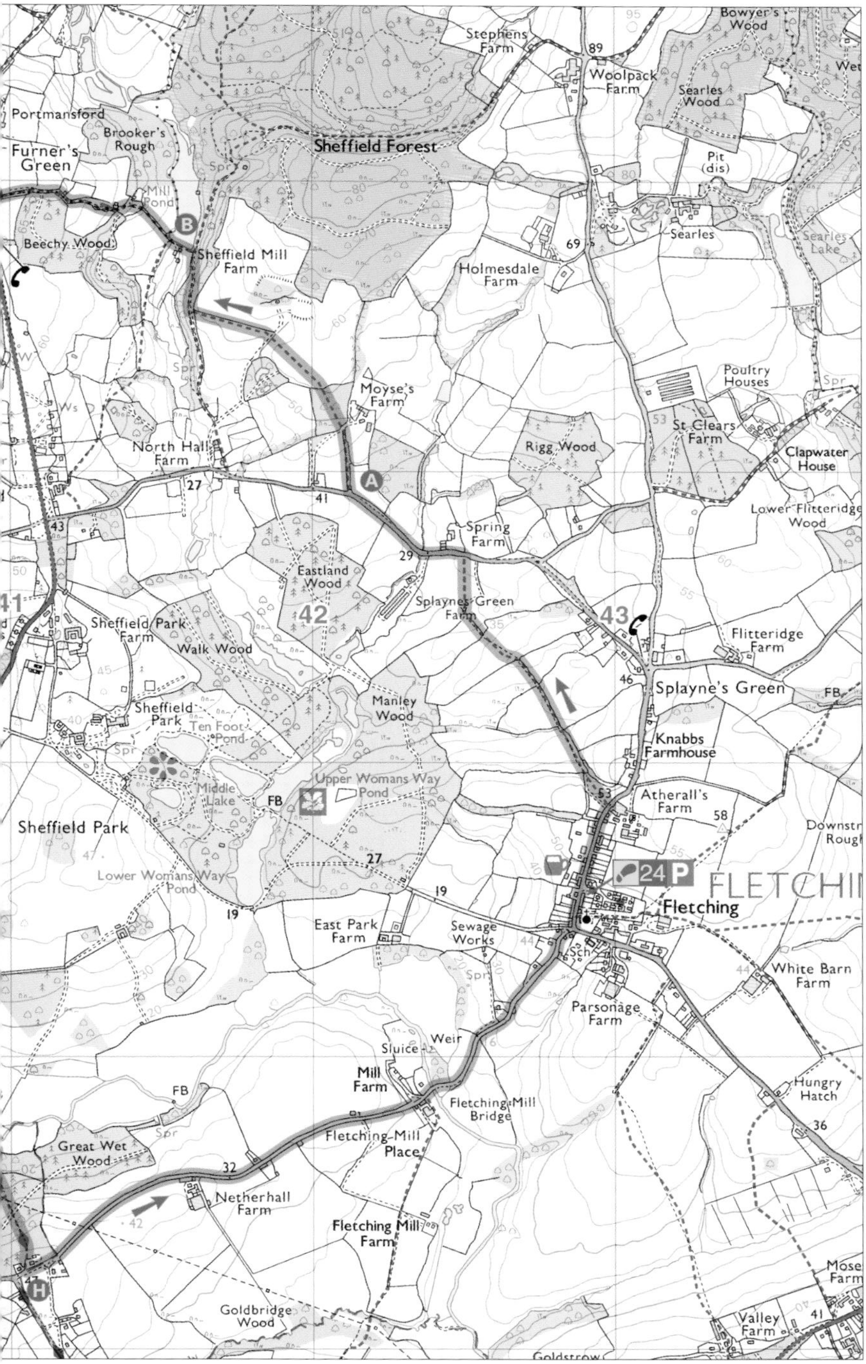

SCALE 1:25000 or 2½ INCHES to 1 MILE 4CM to 1KM

Mill Pond at Sheffield Mill Farm

Northland Farm and keep left along the drive to a lane.

Cross over into King's Wood, fork right and follow the main path into a field. Go straight across, pass to the right of a pond and continue towards the railway. Keep right in the next field and pass beneath the Bluebell Railway. Go through a gate and bear right in 100 yards to a footbridge and gate E.

Bear half-left towards the farm, crossing a footbridge to reach a stile on the field edge. Skirt the farm to a gate, turn left along the road and cross the River Ouse. Pass the **Sloop Inn** and soon follow the Sussex Border Path left along a gravel drive between houses to a gate. Enter woodland and soon fork right to ascend through the trees to a stile. Walk straight across the field ahead, ignoring the footpath right to reach a stile on the edge of Wapsbourne Wood F.

Walk through the wood to a waymarker and turn right, then right again at a wider track. Bear left in a few paces and descend to a stile and field. Turn left to reach a stile by a house. Bear right, go through a gate and soon turn left in front of Wapsbourne Farm to follow the drive out to the A275. Just before the road, turn left along the field edge, drop down to the road and cross over, following the pavement to Sheffield Park Station and the Bluebell Railway G. This 10-mile-long (16km) revived steam railway runs through a picturesque valley route carpeted by a mass of bluebells in spring. There is a **café** and a fascinating locomotive museum with rolling stock dating between 1865 and 1958 at Sheffield Park Station. To visit the National Trust's Sheffield Park Gardens continue north along the pavement. Laid out by Capability Brown in 1775, this beautiful parkland covers 200 acres and has a superb collection of trees and shrubs around five lakes threaded by walks with shimmering vistas, and is best visited for the magnificent autumn colours.

Follow the Ouse Valley Way opposite the entrance, cross a stile and walk beside the River Ouse. Bear right across the rough grassland to follow the field edge into the next field. Go through a gate and soon bear right uphill through woodland. Cross a track to reach a gate H and turn left to follow a quiet lane for 1½ miles (2.4km) back into Fletching. Rest and refuel at **The Griffin Inn**, which has a glorious garden that takes in a 10-mile (16km) view across Sheffield Park to the South Downs.

Cuckmere River and Norton Top from Alfriston

Start	Alfriston	
Distance	9¼ miles (15km)	
Height gain	770 feet (235m)	
Approximate time	4½ hours	
Parking	The Willow long-stay Pay and Display car park on the left of the main road on the northern approach to town	
Route terrain	Field, downland and riverside paths	
Ordnance Survey maps	Landranger 199 (Eastbourne & Hastings), Explorer OL25 (Eastbourne & Beachy Head)	

GPS waypoints

- TQ 521 032
- Ⓐ TQ 519 015
- Ⓑ TQ 509 011
- Ⓒ TQ 488 023
- Ⓓ TQ 497 050
- Ⓔ TQ 507 057
- Ⓕ TQ 512 053
- Ⓖ TQ 518 048

A route that covers riverside and downland inevitably involves a climb or two, but the gradients on this route are reasonably easy and the views outstanding. Half-time refreshment can be taken in village pubs on the homeward leg.

Looking across the Cuckmere Valley to Alfriston church

Turn left out of the car park and walk into the town centre, passing the Market Cross and **The George Inn**. Turn left along a tarmac path beside the United Reformed Church, signed to The Tye, following it slightly left and keeping ahead to reach a footbridge across the Cuckmere River. Cross to the east bank and turn right for Exceat, following the South Downs Way beside the course of the Cuckmere River. Look across the water to see the delicate tracery of the east window of Alfriston Church – often called the 'Cathedral of the Downs'. There are also glimpses of the town's other old buildings – the 14th-century Clergy House was built to cater for parish priests after the Black Death while the **Star Inn** dates from the 15th century and is part timbered.

Look to the left as well and you may see a heron lazily take to the wing from the dykes surrounding the water-meadows. Litlington is reached after 20 minutes or so. Keep to the riverbank path unless you would like to visit the **Plough and Harrow inn** or the village **tearoom**, both up a short footpath on the left. Otherwise, cross the footbridge to the west side of the river.

Follow the path southwards for about 1/4 mile (400m) and, at the first stile, turn right **A** to climb towards the White Horse on Cradle Hill. Keep ahead at a post marking a footpath junction. A little farther on, where the track from Tile Barn joins, it becomes a bridleway that eventually reaches a gate giving on to a road. Do not go through the gate but turn left to follow the grassy path below the road to a stile. Bear right at the top of the enclosed path to reach the High and Over car park on Cradle Hill.

Cross the road and turn right for

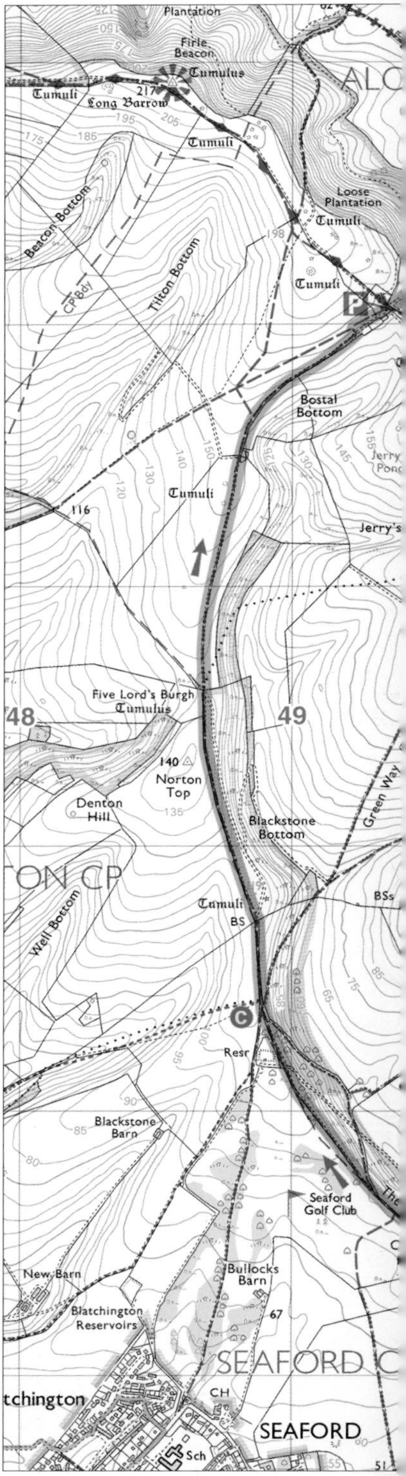

0 200 400 600 800 METRES 1 KILOMETRES
MILES
0 200 400 600 YARDS 1/2

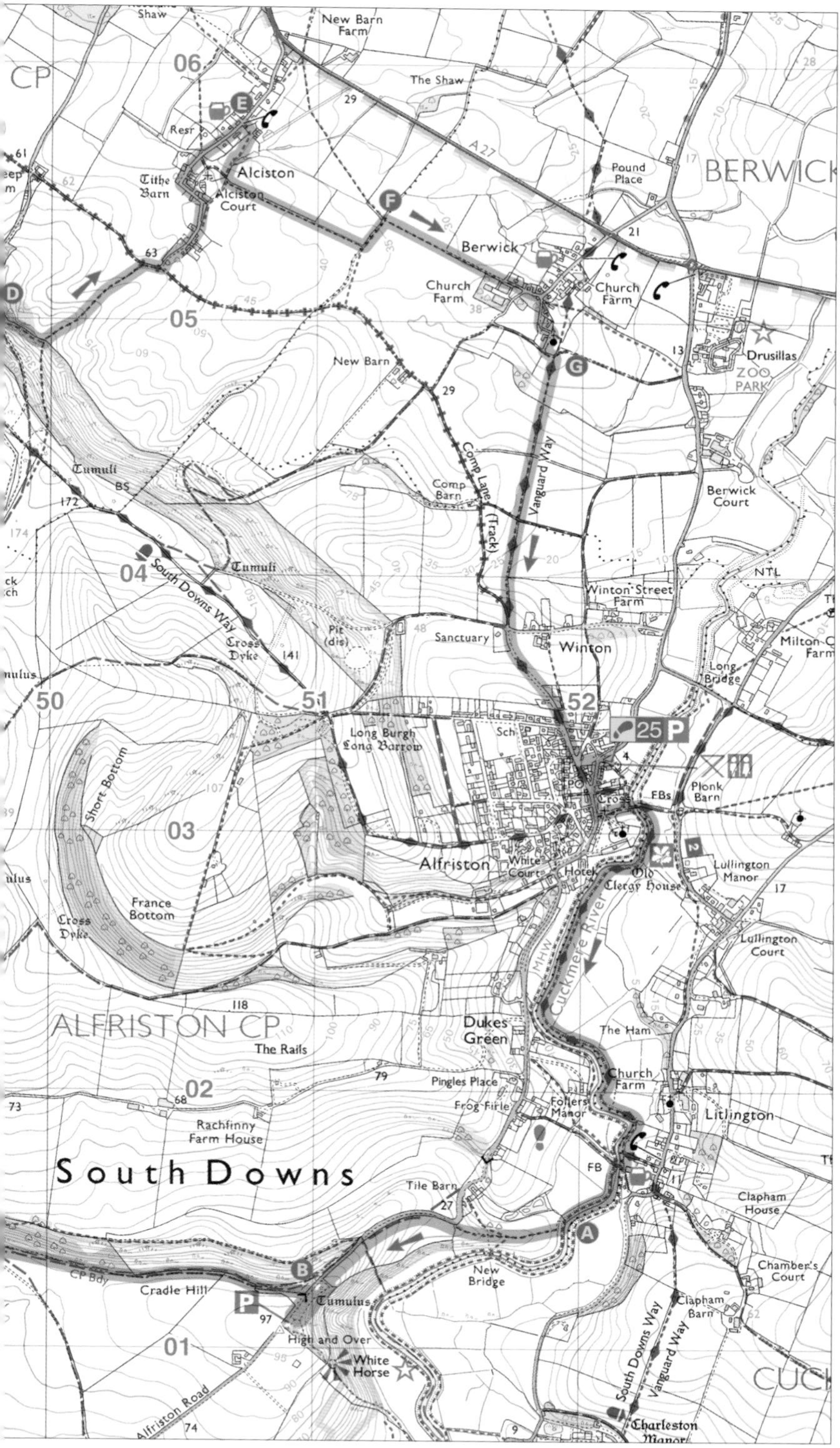

SCALE 1:27777 or 2¼ INCHES to 1 MILE *3.6CM to 1KM*

Across the Weald from above Bopeep Chalk Pit

50 yards to find a stile B on to the National Trust's Frog Firle land. The short foot-path joins the bridleway (known as The Comp) that follows a downland ridge for more than four miles (6.4km) from this point.

After a gate where another bridleway joins, keep right and the way gradually swings to the north along the edge of a golf course. At the end of the latter there is a bench by a crossways C and soon you will have good views eastwards across Blackstone Bottom to rolling countryside beyond. This is an exhilarating walk – after Norton Top the way is level but above Bostal Bottom the land is cultivated and the bridleway joins a farm track.

This joins the road to the car park above Bopeep Chalk Pit, and the stunning view northwards is revealed here. As you descend the road you will find magnificent blackberries that are ripe for eating in late July. Where the road begins a hairpin bend to the left, leave it for a footpath on the right D, going through a gate and then turning left to follow the waymark to Alciston.

The path is shady through woodland but, when it emerges from the trees, climb the stile on the left and descend along the edge of a field, keeping trees to your right. Turn right at a track and then left into the village passing a beautiful flint Tithe Barn and walking past the drive to the church. In the village centre, by the telephone box and parish notice board E, turn right, cross a stile and then turn right at the barn. Now make for the left-hand edge of the churchyard wall. Cross a stile and turn right, then almost immediately left. Follow the field edge to a T-junction, turn left and then right F to follow a path between fields and soon join a concrete track into Berwick. At yet another T-junction you can either turn left for a refreshment stop at the **Cricketers Inn** or go right to continue on the route past the south side of the church.

Turn right here G to take a footpath heading southwards between fields. Keep ahead when it meets a lane and turn left through the short-stay car park to reach the car park on the other side of the main street.

Downland Walk from Telscombe

Start	Telscombe, 4 miles (6.4km) south of Lewes
Distance	9½ miles (15.3km)
Height gain	1,050 feet (320m)
Approximate time	4½ hours
Parking	On the broad verge beyond the youth hostel at south end of village
Route terrain	Downland tracks
Ordnance Survey maps	Landranger 198 (Brighton & Lewes), Explorer OL11 (Brighton & Hove)

GPS waypoints

- Start TQ 404 032
- A TQ 399 033
- B TQ 383 052
- C TQ 378 050
- D TQ 378 058
- E TQ 367 073
- F TQ 379 079
- G TQ 391 067
- H TQ 413 048

Although it is only four miles (6.4km) from Lewes, little Telscombe feels like the most remote of all downland villages. You are more likely to meet horse-riders than other walkers on the first part of the route, which leads ever deeper into the heart of the downs and mainly stays on the ridge. When it descends, the wayside wild flowers are a wonderful recompense.

The road runs up to a gate and cattle-grid. Take the bridleway to the right, a track leading towards a pair of houses. The sea is to the left and the downs extend in every other direction. Turn right **A** before reaching the drives to the two houses on to a bridleway that heads north, by a fence. It joins a track opposite a modern installation to the left. Keep ahead where a footpath goes to the right and a bridleway leaves to the left. There is a good view to the left over Saltdean before you pass a derelict shed on the right where a barn is now visible in the fields to the left. This is Sussex downland at its best, and in spring and summer hosts of butterflies rise from the wayside flowers, even though the fields are cropped. There is a prominent monument by the path where John Harvey died suddenly on June 20, 1819. He was a notable country gentleman from Bedfordshire and had probably come to Brighton believing that the new resort would be good for his health.

Pass the memorial and soon you reach the next junction **B**. Bear left to descend towards a cattle-shed. Climb a slope to a gate and turn right **C** on a bridleway, which is part of a South Downs Circular Walk (but a different one to this).

The track heads into a deserted landscape with all habitation soon lost to sight. At a large stand of sycamore and ash trees, turn right **D** to head for roofless cattle-sheds. Keep ahead at the bridleway junction by the sheds to pass below a clump of trees and go through a gate, now walking on a grassy path on the right-hand side of a dry valley. The wild flowers are spectacular and skylarks sing above.

At the top of Falmer Bottom the bridleway goes through a gate by a National Nature Reserve sign and ahead on a track. This passes through part of Castle Hill National Nature Reserve, where the steep slopes have never been cultivated by machinery and have a wide variety of chalk-loving plants, many of them rare. The one steep climb of the walk comes with the ascent of Newmarket Hill, up the coomb from Falmer Bottom. Go through the gate at the top and turn right E to join Jugg's Road (an ancient track that runs directly to Lewes) and the South Downs Way. This stretch of grassy walking is a highlight of the route, with the sea in the distance to the right and a vast expanse of downland revealed on the left beyond the A27 and the railway. The modern pattern of vast fields is only relieved by a few smaller ones.

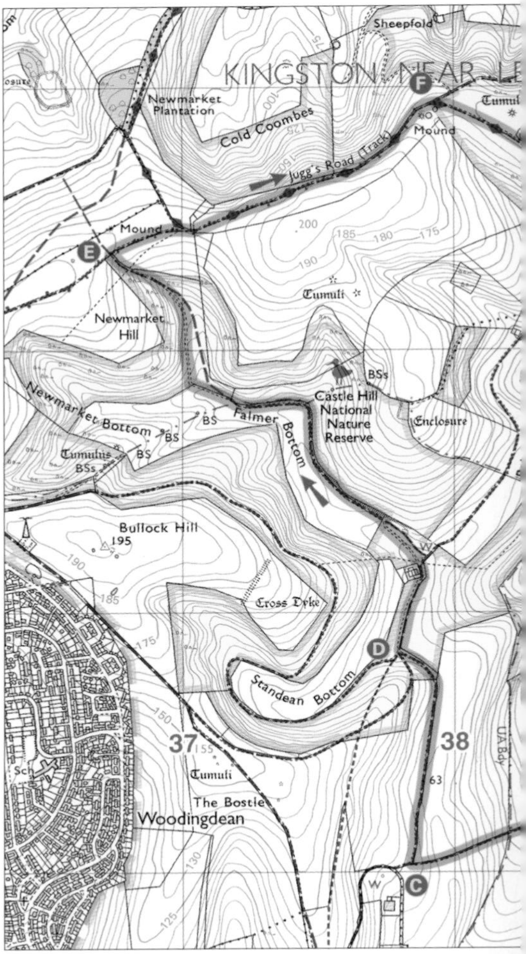

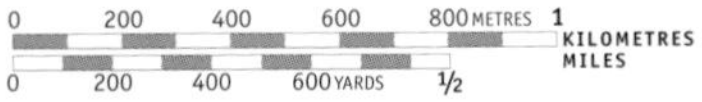

On reaching a gate and galvanised gate on Jugg's Road, go straight on for Lewes or branch right F to follow the South Downs Way. Continue for some time, meet Dencher Road joining from the left and 200 yards farther on a gate takes the path to the other side of the fence. After a bridleway (coming from near the Harvey monument) joins at the crest, turn left G on to a concrete road that makes for two miles (3.2km) of easygoing walking with views of the Seven Sisters ahead in the distance.

Keep ahead when the concrete track meets another one to follow a bridleway along the field edge. Cross White Way and climb Mill Hill and then cross a drive going to a house to stay with the South Downs Way. At the bottom, turn right to leave the long-distance path H and walk through the farmyard. The track winds up through Cricketing Bottom before bending left at a waymark, then swinging right to climb steeply to the lane leading to Telscombe. Keep right and return to the village. ●

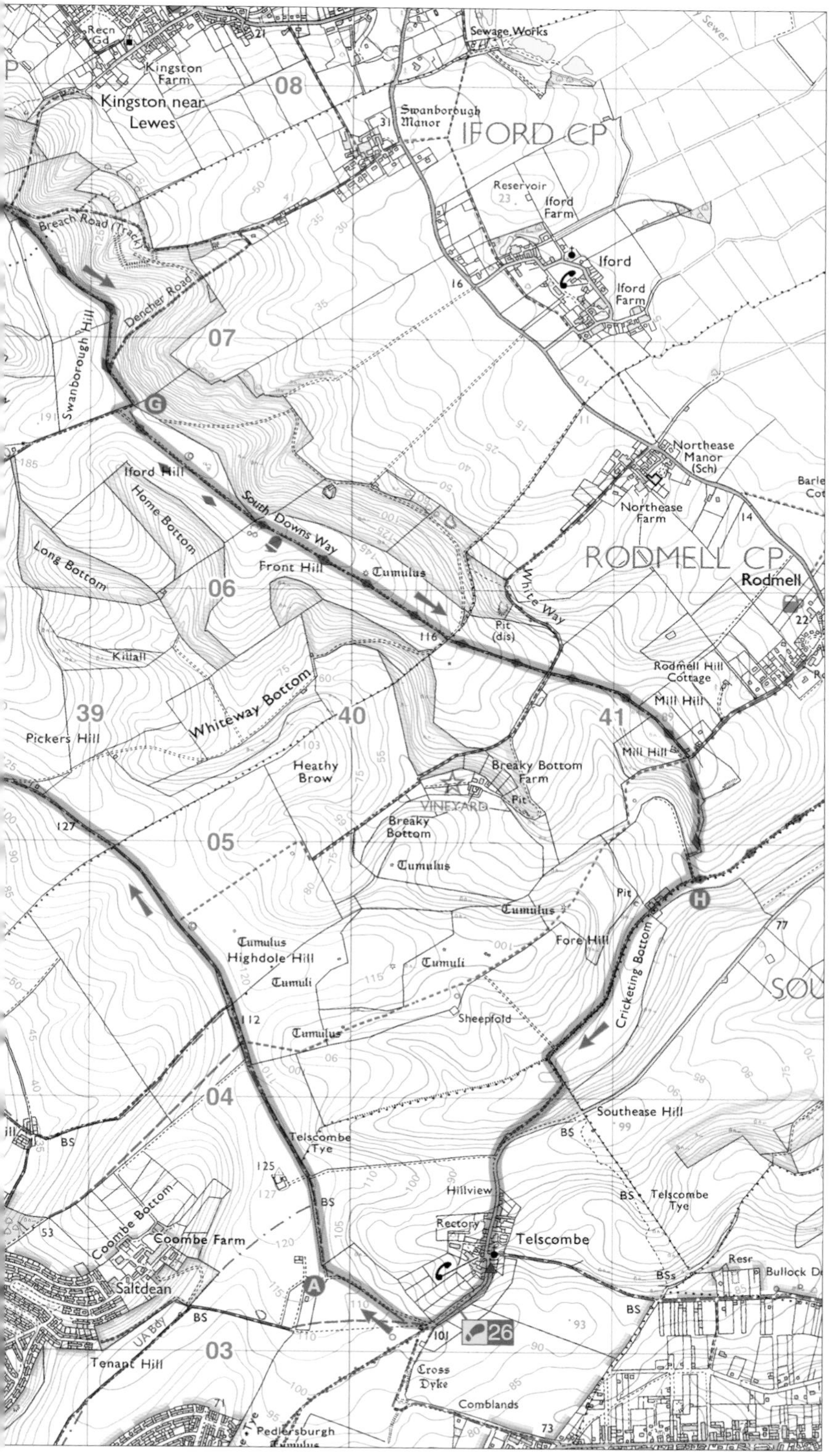

SCALE 1:27777 or 2¼ INCHES to 1 MILE 3.6CM to 1KM

Ditchling Beacon, Clayton Windmills and Chattri Memorial

Start	Foot of Ditchling Beacon
Distance	9 miles (14.5km). Shorter version 6 miles (9.4km)
Height gain	1,565ft (475m). Shorter version 810ft (245m)
Approximate time	5 hours. Shorter version 3 hours
Parking	Underhill Lane car park at the foot of Ditchling Beacon; or National Trust car park at Ditchling Beacon (Pay and Display)
Route terrain	Downland paths and tracks; quiet tarmac lane
Ordnance Survey maps	Landranger 198 (Brighton & Lewes), Explorer OL11 (Brighton & Hove)

GPS waypoints

Start	TQ 325 137
A	TQ 330 131
B	TQ 314 115
C	TQ 309 117
D	TQ 304 110
E	TQ 302 134

Ditchling Beacon is highly popular with the public as it has a car park more or less at its summit. That's the starting point for the shorter version of the walk but the longer one begins at the car park at the foot of Ditchling Beacon, the splendid views from the top all the more rewarding for having earned them. Both walks take in the Clayton Windmills, known as Jack and Jill, the pair a distinctive landmark on the South Downs, while the longer route also includes a visit to the Chattri Indian War Memorial, a very atmospheric spot on the Downs.

From the Underhill Lane car park follow the footpath that climbs up through the woodland, passing a stile on the right (open access downland the other side) and kissing-gate on the left (Ditchling Beacon Nature Reserve sign). Keep ahead to reach a fork where the path divides on the other side of a kissing-gate (ignore the gate on the left just before it). *Alternatively, for better views, you could climb over the stile and walk up the grass alongside the fence until you reach the next stile on the left, with a few steps up to it. Cross over and head on up to cross another stile, rejoining the main path at the fork.* Go through the kissing-gate and bear left, soon emerging from the trees. The gradient eases and then there's a steady climb up a grassy bank to the top of the Downs. Keep alongside the fence on the left nearing the top, eventually meeting the South Downs Way (SDW) just west of the Ditchling Beacon car park. Turn right. A path to the left leads to the Beacon itself and the trig point: a worthwhile detour. *For the shorter walk starting from the Ditchling Beacon car park, go through the gate at the top and follow the chalky track (SDW) which climbs westwards to join the longer route.*

Continue along the SDW for a short distance to a four-armed fingerpost and gate on the left **A**. Turn left through the gate and follow the bridleway southwards, enjoying views along the South Downs to the west and over Hogtrough Bottom below to the right. Keep ahead at a waymark post on the left, now descending more steeply, the bridleway enclosed by fences either side. On reaching the open grass, bear right to carry on down to the lovely valley, North Bottom. At the bottom just past some trees go through a gate and continue along the valley. Before long a track can be seen ahead running parallel to the fence on the other side. Continue to a bridle gate and go right through this and left along the track, branching right after 200 yards onto a track which climbs the right side of the valley. At a fingerpost keep ahead (right fork) on the track (permissive bridleway), continuing uphill, then down via a gate to another gate to meet a bridleway on the west side of the farmyard at Lower Standean **B**.

Turn right and follow the bridleway up, ignoring turns. The track bears right past a flint and brick farm building, swings round to the left and then bends right to the top of the rise and a fingerpost. The

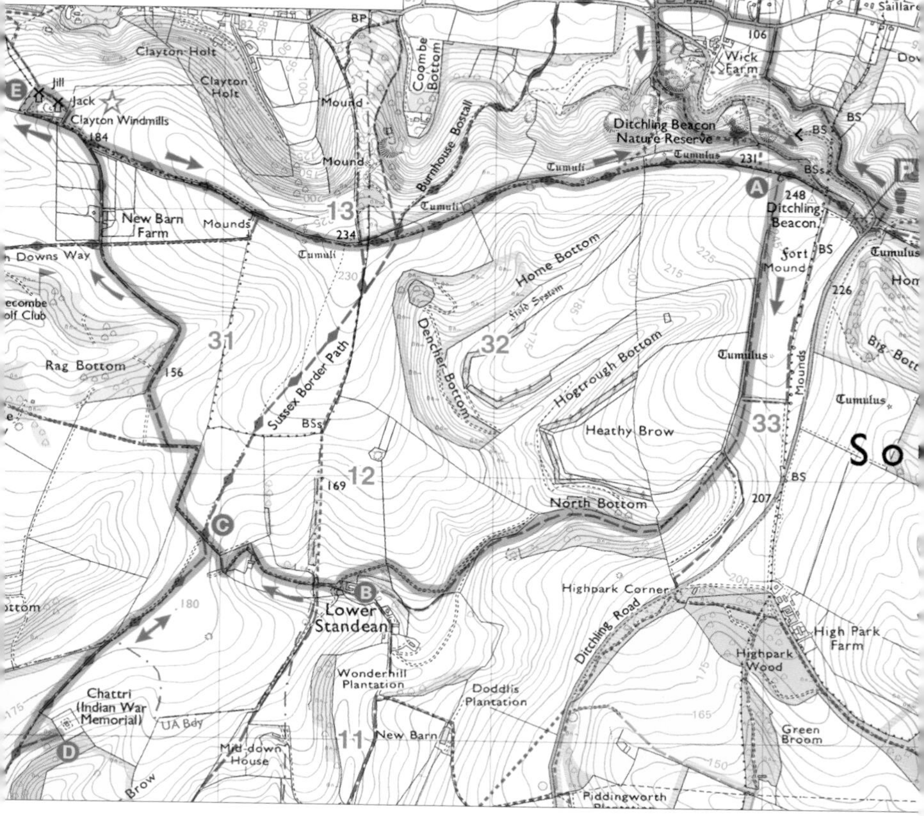

Chattri Memorial

Sussex Border Path crosses here Ⓒ.

While the shorter walk keeps ahead here, the longer version turns left to follow the bridleway southwards to the Chattri memorial (3/4 mile/1.2km each way). It's a level walk, initially through an open field towards the large clump of trees visible ahead and thereafter alongside a fence on the right to reach a gate and information panel. Go through the gate and turn immediately left downhill to go through the second of two gates, signed the Chattri Memorial, which was built in honour of First World War Indian soldiers. The wounded were hospitalised in Brighton, and the Hindus and Sikhs who died were cremated here. Accessible only on foot, it's a peaceful and atmospheric spot Ⓓ.

Retrace your steps to waypoint Ⓒ. Turn left along the field edge to a gate and right beside the fence, and then left leaving the hedge heading west. After about 100 yards turn right and follow the bridleway northwards, descending to pass round the eastern end of the Pyecombe Golf Club course and back uphill to meet the SDW at a path intersection. Joining the SDW, keep ahead on the track passing New Barn Farm. At the next junction the SDW turns sharp right – the return leg of the walk. But first turn left and walk down the track to the car park on the right Ⓔ, which provides a good view of the windmills, especially the white one, Jill, a restored 19th century working windmill, open to the public most Sunday afternoons from May to September. Black Jack windmill is in private ownership. The windmills' car park also affords fine views over the Sussex Weald.

Go through the gap in the far right corner of the car park and follow the fenced path round the perimeter of the windmills' enclosure rejoining the main track and turning left. At the SDW, fork left along the ridge-top track, which ascends gradually to reach a gate and fingerpost on the left at the top. Continuing on the SDW, go through the bridle gate ahead following the track gently down to another gate, Ditchling Beacon in the distance ahead. On the other side of the gate on the left is Burnt House dew pond. Dew ponds, as they are called (despite most of the water coming from rainfall), were created by farmers to provide drinking water for livestock. Another is passed on the right a little further on. Continue along the broad grassy ridge, the fence now a little below on the left, to reach another gate. Go through this and carry on back to the Ditchling Beacon car park, where the shorter walk finishes.

For the longer route, keep to the left of the car park, cross the road with care and turn immediately left down the path/bridleway alongside the road, soon parting company with the road. The path descends through trees and near the bottom becomes a track leading to Underhill Lane. Turn left along the quiet lane to the crossroads and go over to the car park just beyond.

Lewes, Balmer Down and the River Ouse

Start	Lewes
Distance	12 miles (19.2km)
Height gain	1,590 feet (485m)
Approximate time	6 hours
Parking	Lewes – Brook Street/Spring Gardens Pay and Display car park
Route terrain	Town streets, downland, woodland and riverside paths
Ordnance Survey maps	Landranger 198 (Brighton & Lewes), Explorer OL11 (Brighton & Hove)

GPS waypoints

- TQ 416 104
- A TQ 408 095
- B TQ 370 074
- C TQ 373 087
- D TQ 364 115
- E TQ 370 125
- F TQ 400 121
- G TQ 402 116

The walk begins and ends at Lewes, a town with an abundance of old buildings, including a notable castle. Once out of the town, the way lies over tracts of lonely downland where the walking, though often energetic, cannot fail to be enjoyable.

Turn right out of the car park and walk up North Street, bearing right into West Street which takes you to Mount Pleasant. Turn left up the hill opposite the **Elephant and Castle** pub to climb Castle Banks, bending right at the top heading towards Lewes Castle. Continue past the bollards and the bowling green on the left. Once at Castle Gate, (the main entrance to the castle), pass through to emerge into the High Street and turn right.

At the top of the High Street, opposite the **Pelham Arms** and just before the church, turn left down a lane, which becomes a footpath, passing the County Hall car park to reach Rotten Row. Turn right, then fork left down St Pancras Road and turn right at the end. Keep ahead past the **Swan Inn** and bear right (A) down Jugg's Road, which soon swings left to cross the bypass by a bridge. Once over the bridge the road begins to climb, and beyond the houses it becomes a track, a field on the left.

Keep ahead through a gate across the open grassland, at the far end passing on the right the six-sweep Ashcombe windmill, a 21st century reconstruction of the original destroyed in a gale in 1916. At Kingston Hollow cross the lane onto the access road opposite to Kingstonridge and at the end keep ahead along the track, which begins to climb gently. Bear right at the fork, the track now ascending quite steeply. Keep straight on at the top, with the fence on the right and pass through a gate.

The grassy track runs just below the ridge, heading towards a transmitter mast. However, well before reaching the mast, go through a gate next to a gas pumping station and immediately turn right to leave Jugg's Road (B), onto a bridleway heading north-west (South Downs Way). Falmer is seen ahead as the path drops down to Newmarket Plantation, where it swings to the right. Descend the track until you see a small gate to the left of a fingerpost **C**. Branch left through the gate still following the South Downs Way and descend quite steeply. At the bottom it continues alongside a field on the left, follows it round to the left, turns right under the railway line and left, parallel to the main road. It eventually joins a road leading up to a bridge crossing the A27. Turn right after the bridge to pass Housedean Farm, and at the end of the wall turn left to climb the steps to a gate. This bridleway takes you up Long Hill and then drops down through Bunkershill Plantation, and then emerges onto downland again. It veers right to begin a gentle climb to reach a gate and a junction with a footpath. Turn left here and climb over Balmer Down. The pylon at the top of the hill is in sight for about one mile (1.6km). Just beyond this a bridleway is met **D**; turn right onto it.

A level stretch follows on a good track. At a five-way junction **E** turn right (east) through the gate towards Lewes, and after about 90 yards fork left up to the Blackcap trig point. Just after this take the left fork gently descending the grassy slopes and keeping above the wooded northern escarpment. Pass to the right of the beacon atop Mount Harry and continue down the grassy strip to a gate. Carry on down through the next field towards the trees. At the fence corner the bridleway continues beside the fence on the right, trees on the left. Go through a gate and continue to a junction by a waymark post.

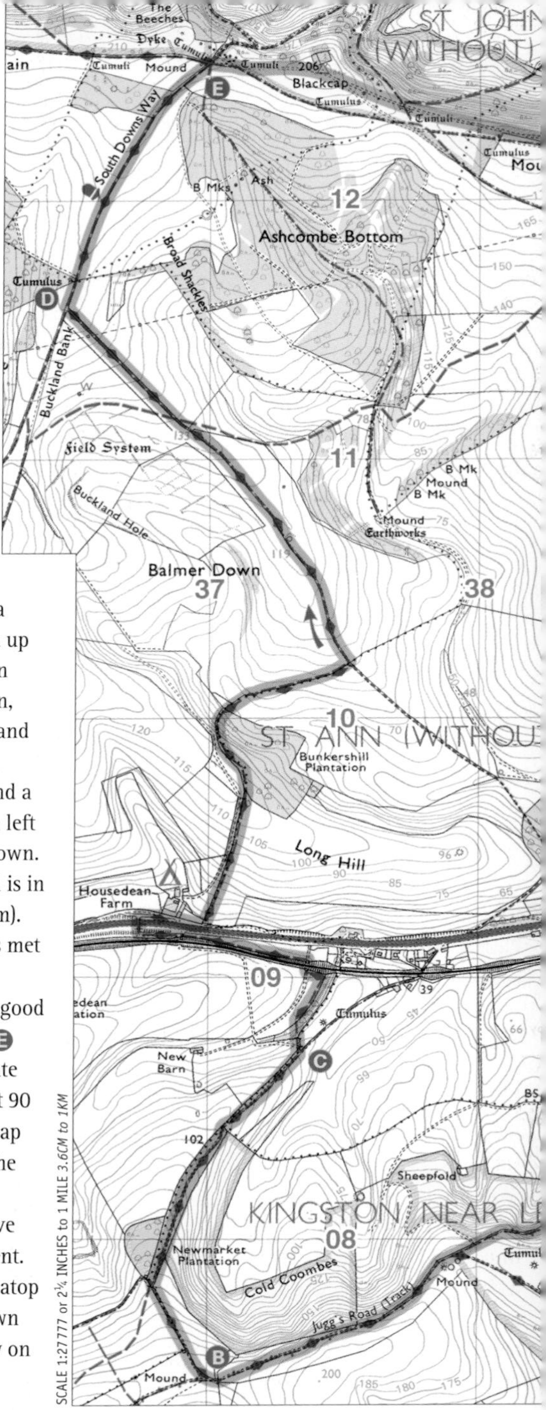

Turn left into the wood and bear right following the bridleway through the trees. Go through a gate and then another one and turn left. The path emerges from the

wood and descends a chalky track to the main road.

Cross the road and turn left, then right onto the lane to Hamsey, the **Blacksmith's Arms** at Offham on the opposite side of the main road. Just past the church where the road bends left (F) turn right onto a byway through the wood. Look for a gate on the left (G) which gives onto a grassy, embanked path to the railway. Go through a gate, then under the railway and continue to the riverbank. Turn right and walk by the River Ouse back to Lewes. At the river footbridge, turn right, walk past the swimming pool by an ornamental canal to Brook Street and turn left to the car park.

0 200 400 600 800 METRES 1 KILOMETRES
0 200 400 600 YARDS 1/2 MILES

Further Information

Walking Safety

Although the reasonably gentle countryside that is the subject of this book offers no real dangers to walkers at any time of the year, it is still advisable to take sensible precautions and follow certain well-tried guidelines.

Always take with you both warm and waterproof clothing and sufficient food and drink. Wear suitable footwear, such as strong walking boots or shoes that give a good grip over stony ground, on slippery slopes and in muddy conditions. Try to obtain a local weather forecast and bear it in mind before you start. Do not be afraid to abandon your proposed route and return to your starting point in the event of a sudden and unexpected deterioration in the weather.

All the walks described in this book will be safe to do, given due care and respect, even during the winter. Indeed, a crisp, fine winter day often provides perfect walking conditions, with firm ground underfoot and a clarity unique to this time of the year. The most difficult hazard likely to be encountered is mud, especially when walking along woodland and field paths, farm tracks and bridleways – the latter in particular can often get churned up by cyclists and horses. In summer, an additional difficulty may be narrow and overgrown paths, particularly along the edges of cultivated fields. Neither should constitute a major problem provided that the appropriate footwear is worn.

The Ramblers

No organisation works more actively to protect and extend the rights and interests of walkers in the countryside than the Ramblers. Its aims are clear: to foster a greater knowledge, love and care of the countryside; to assist in the protection and enhancement of public rights of way and areas of natural beauty; to work for greater public access to the countryside; and to encourage more people to take up rambling as a healthy, recreational leisure activity.

It was founded in 1935 and the Ramblers has played a key role in preserving and developing the national footpath network, supporting the creation of national parks and encouraging the designation and waymarking of long-distance routes.

Our freedom of access to the countryside, now enshrined in legislation, is still in its early years and requires constant vigilance. But over and above this there will always be the problem of footpaths being illegally obstructed, disappearing through lack of use, or being extinguished by housing or road construction.

It is to meet such problems and dangers that the Ramblers exists and represents the interests of all walkers. The address to write to for information on the Ramblers and how to become a member is given on page 95.

Walkers and the Law

The Countryside and Rights of Way Act (CRoW Act 2000) gives a public right of access in England and Wales to land mapped as open country (mountain, moor, heath and down) or registered common land. These areas are known as *open access land*, and include land around the coastline, known as *coastal margin.*

Where You Can Go

Rights of Way

Prior to the introduction of the CRoW Act, walkers could only legally access the countryside along public rights of way. These are either 'footpaths' (for walkers only) or 'bridleways' (for walkers, riders on horseback and pedal cyclists). A third category called 'Byways open to all traffic' (BOATs), is used by motorised vehicles as well as those using non-mechanised transport. Mainly they are green lanes, farm

Countryside Access Charter

Your rights of way are:

- public footpaths – on foot only. Sometimes waymarked in yellow
- bridle-ways – on foot, horseback and pedal cycle. Sometimes waymarked in blue
- byways (usually old roads), most 'roads used as public paths' and, of course, public roads – all traffic has the right of way

Use maps, signs and waymarks to check rights of way. Ordnance Survey Explorer and Landranger maps show most public rights of way

On rights of way you can:

- take a pram, pushchair or wheelchair if practicable
- take a dog (on a lead or under close control)
- take a short route round an illegal obstruction or remove it sufficiently to get past

You have a right to go for recreation to:

- public parks and open spaces – on foot
- most commons near older towns and cities – on foot and sometimes on horseback
- private land where the owner has a formal agreement with the local authority

In addition you can use the following by local or established custom or consent, but ask for advice if you are unsure:

- many areas of open country, such as moorland, fell and coastal areas, especially those in the care of the National Trust, and some commons
- some woods and forests, especially those owned by the Forestry Commission
- country parks and picnic sites
- most beaches
- canal towpaths
- some private paths and tracks Consent sometimes extends to horse-riding and cycling

For your information:

- county councils and London boroughs maintain and record rights of way, and register commons
- obstructions, dangerous animals, harassment and misleading signs on rights of way are illegal and you should report them to the county council
- paths across fields can be ploughed, but must normally be reinstated within two weeks
- landowners can require you to leave land to which you have no right of access
- motor vehicles are normally permitted only on roads, byways and some 'roads used as public paths'

and estate roads, although occasionally they will be found crossing mountainous area.

Rights of way are marked on Ordnance Survey maps. Look for the green broken lines on the Explorer maps, or the red dashed lines on Landranger maps.

The term 'right of way' means exactly what it says. It gives a right of passage over what, for the most part, is private land. Under pre-CRoW legislation walkers were required to keep to the line of the right of way and not stray onto land on either side. If you did inadvertently wander off the right of way, either because of faulty map reading or because the route was not clearly indicated on the ground, you were technically trespassing.

Local authorities have a legal obligation to ensure that rights of way are kept clear and free of obstruction, and are signposted where they leave metalled roads. The duty of local authorities to install signposts extends to the placing of signs along a path or way, but only where the authority considers it necessary to have a signpost or waymark to assist persons unfamiliar with the locality.

CRoW Access Rights

Access Land

As well as being able to walk on existing rights of way, under CRoW legislation you have access to large areas of open land and, under further legislation, a right of coastal access, which is being implemented by Natural England, giving for the first time the right of access around all England's open coast. This includes plans for an England Coast Path (ECP) which will run for 2,795 miles (4,500 kilometres). A corresponding Wales Coast Path has been open since 2012.

Coastal access rights apply within the coastal margin (including along the ECP) unless the land falls into a category of excepted land or is subject to local restrictions, exclusions or diversions.

You can of course continue to use rights of way to cross access land, but you can lawfully leave the path and wander at will in these designated areas.

Where to Walk

Access Land is shown on Ordnance Survey Explorer maps by a light yellow tint surrounded by a pale orange border. New orange coloured 'i' symbols on the maps will show the location of permanent access information boards installed by the access authorities. Coastal Margin is shown on Ordnance Survey Explorer maps by a pink tint.

Restrictions

The right to walk on access land may lawfully be restricted by landowners. Landowners can, for any reason, restrict access for up to 28 days in any year. They cannot however close the land:

- on bank holidays;
- for more than four Saturdays and Sundays in a year;
- on any Saturday from 1 June to 11 August; or
- on any Sunday from 1 June to the end of September.

They have to provide local authorities with five working days' notice before the date of closure unless the land involved is an area of less than five hectares or the closure is for less than four hours. In these cases landowners only need to provide two hours' notice.

Whatever restrictions are put into place on access land they have no effect on existing rights of way, and you can continue to walk on them.

Dogs

Dogs can be taken on access land, but must be kept on leads of two metres or less between 1 March and 31 July, and at all times where they are near livestock. In addition landowners may impose a ban on all dogs from fields where lambing takes place for up to six weeks in any year. Dogs may be banned from moorland used for grouse shooting and breeding for up to five years.

In the main, walkers following the routes in this book will continue to follow existing rights of way, but a knowledge and understanding of the law as it affects walkers, plus the ability to distinguish access land marked on the maps, will enable anyone who wishes to depart from paths that cross access land either to take a shortcut, to enjoy a view or to explore.

General Obstructions

Obstructions can sometimes cause a problem on a walk and the most common of these is where the path across a field has been ploughed over. It is legal for a farmer to plough up a path provided that it is restored within two weeks. This does not always happen and you are faced with the dilemma of following the line of the path, even if this means treading on crops, or walking round the edge of the field. Although the latter course of action seems the most sensible, it does mean that you would be trespassing.

Other obstructions can vary from overhanging vegetation to wire fences across the path, locked gates or even a cattle feeder on the path.

Use common sense. If you can get round the obstruction without causing damage, do so. Otherwise only remove as much of the obstruction as is necessary to secure passage.

If the right of way is blocked and cannot be followed, there is a long-standing view that in such circumstances there is a right to deviate, but this cannot wholly be relied on. Although it is accepted in law that highways (and that includes rights of way) are for the public service, and if the usual track is impassable, it is for the general good that people should be entitled to pass into another line. However, this should not be taken as indicating a right to deviate whenever a way becomes impassable. If in doubt, retreat.

Report obstructions to the local authority and/or The Ramblers.

Useful Organisations

Campaign for National Parks
Tel. 020 7981 0890
www.cnp.org.uk

Campaign to Protect Rural England
Tel. 020 7981 2800
www.cpre.org.uk

English Heritage
Tel. 0370 333 1181
www.english-heritage.org.uk

Forestry Commission England
Tel. 0300 067 4420
www.forestry.gov.uk

National Trust
Tel. 0344 800 1895
www.nationaltrust.org.uk

Natural England
Tel. 0300 060 3900
www.gov.uk/government/organisations/natural-england

Ordnance Survey
Tel. 03456 050505
www.ordnancesurvey.co.uk

Ramblers
2nd Floor, Camelford House
87-90 Albert Embankment,
London
SE1 7TW
Tel. 020 7339 8500
www.ramblers.org.uk

Youth Hostels Association
Trevelyan House,
Dimple Road, Matlock
Derbyshire
DE4 3YH
Tel. 01629 592700
www.yha.org.uk

Traveline
Tel. 0871 200 2233

National Train Enquiry Line
Tel. 03457 484950

Tourist Information Centres
Bexhill: 01797 229049
Eastbourne: 01323 415415
Hastings: 01424 451111
Lewes: 01273 483448
Rye: 01797 226696
Seaford: 01323 897426

East Sussex County Council
Roads and paths
Tel. 0345 6080193
www.eastsussex.gov.uk

Ordnance Survey maps of South Downs National Park & East Sussex

East Sussex and the South Downs are covered by Ordnance Survey 1:50 000 scale (1¼ inches to 1 mile or 2cm to 1km) Landranger map sheets 187, 188, 189, 198 and 199. These all-purpose maps are packed with information to help you explore the area. Viewpoints, picnic sites, places of interest and caravan and camping sites are shown, as well as public rights of way information such as footpaths and bridleways. To examine East Sussex and the South Downs in more detail, and especially if you are planning walks, Ordnance Survey Explorer maps at 1:25 000 (2½ inches to 1 mile or 4cm to 1km) are ideal:

OL11	Brighton & Hove
OL25	Eastbourne & Beachy Head
124	Hastings & Bexhill
125	Romney Marsh, Rye & Winchelsea
OL34	Crawley & Horsham
135	Ashdown Forest
136	High Weald, Royal Tunbridge Wells